C000247262

The Secretary Bird

A Comedy

William Douglas Home

A SAMUEL FRENCH ACTING EDITION

SAMUEL FRENCH

FOUNDED 1830

SAMUELFRENCH-LONDON.CO.UK
SAMUELFRENCH.COM

Copyright © 1969 by William Douglas Home

All Rights Reserved

THE SECRETARY BIRD is fully protected under the copyright laws of the British Commonwealth, including Canada, the United States of America, and all other countries of the Copyright Union. All rights, including professional and amateur stage productions, recitation, lecturing, public reading, motion picture, radio broadcasting, television and the rights of translation into foreign languages are strictly reserved.

ISBN 978-0-573-01387-4

www.samuelfrench-london.co.uk

www.samuelfrench.com

FOR AMATEUR PRODUCTION ENQUIRIES

UNITED KINGDOM AND WORLD EXCLUDING NORTH AMERICA

plays@SamuelFrench-London.co.uk

020 7255 4302/01

Each title is subject to availability from Samuel French,

depending upon country of performance.

CAUTION: Professional and amateur producers are hereby warned that *THE SECRETARY BIRD* is subject to a licensing fee. Publication of this play does not imply availability for performance. Both amateurs and professionals considering a production are strongly advised to apply to the appropriate agent before starting rehearsals, advertising, or booking a theatre. A licensing fee must be paid whether the title is presented for charity or gain and whether or not admission is charged.

The professional rights in this play are controlled by Samuel French Ltd, 52 Fitzroy Street, London, W1T 5JR.

No one shall make any changes in this title for the purpose of production. No part of this book may be reproduced, stored in a retrieval system, or transmitted in any form, by any means, now known or yet to be invented, including mechanical, electronic, photocopying, recording, videotaping, or otherwise, without the prior written permission of the publisher. No one shall upload this title, or part of this title, to any social media websites.

The right of William Douglas Home to be identified as author of this work has been asserted by him in accordance with Section 77 of the Copyright, Designs and Patents Act 1988

THE SECRETARY BIRD

First produced by Anthony Roye at the Mowlem Theatre, Swanage, on the 9th May 1967, with the following cast of characters:

(in order of their appearance)

HUGH WALFORD	*Anthony Roye*
LIZ WALFORD	*Patrica Leslie*
MRS GRAY	*Betty Woolfe*
MOLLY FORSYTH	*Dona Martyn*
JOHN BROWNLOW	*Robert Dean*

Subsequently produced by John Gale, for Volcano Productions, at the Savoy Theatre, London, on 16th October 1968, with the following cast of characters:

(in order of their appearance)

HUGH WALFORD	*Kenneth More*
LIZ WALFORD	*Jane Downs*
MRS GRAY	*Katherine Parr*
MOLLY FORSYTH	*Judith Arthy*
JOHN BROWNLOW	*Terence Longdon*

The play directed by Philip Dudley

Setting by Hutchinson Scott

The action of the play passes in the living-room of the Walford's country house

ACT I

SCENE 1 Friday night
SCENE 2 Saturday morning

ACT II

SCENE 1 Saturday night
SCENE 2 Sunday morning

Time—the present

ACT I

Scene i

SCENE—*The living-room of the Walford's country home. Friday night. It is a charming room, much lived in, comfortable, well-furnished, homely. Double doors in a small alcove up* LC *lead to the hall, and french windows in a bay* R *to the garden. Down* L *is a recessed fireplace.*

When the CURTAIN *rises,* HUGH *and* LIZ, *his wife, are sitting at a card table* LC *playing Racing Demon.* HUGH *is on a chair above the table,* LIZ *on the sofa* R *of it. They play quite slowly as the Curtain rises, then they quicken steadily, and then the pace gets fast and furious. Eventually* HUGH *cries "Out!". He gathers all the cards together from the middle of the table and divides the packs, one colour for himself and one for* LIZ.

HUGH. How many in your "talon", darling?

LIZ (*who has just counted them*) Seven.

HUGH. Bad luck. I had a damned lucky run. How many are you? (*He counts his output as he divides the cards*)

LIZ (*counting*) Nine.

HUGH. That makes you eighty-four. I'm thirty-eight. That's—eight and five—thirteen. And carry one—four—four and six—ten—one hundred and three. I've done it. One game all, my darling. Now for the decider. Damned close games, they've been. Let's see, you were a hundred and ten in the first game. I was eighty-seven. And, in this one, I'm a hundred and three, and you're eighty-seven. Cut to me, my darling.

LIZ. Do you mind if we don't—not tonight. I'm feeling tired.

HUGH (*noting her strange mood, but providing an excuse*) Poor darling. Yes—of course, you must be. Up and down from London in the same day. Have a drink? (*He rises*)

LIZ. Oh, all right—a small whisky.

HUGH (*moving to the drinks table up* C) That's right. (*He pours*) And I'll have a large one. Beats me why you never took the train, instead of that damned car. It's sixty miles each way. Where did you lunch?

LIZ. At the hairdresser.

HUGH. Sandwiches, I'll bet.

LIZ. Of course.

HUGH. Under the drier?

LIZ. Where else?

HUGH. Never ring your wife up at the hairdresser a fellow once told me—because she won't be there.

LIZ. Did you ring me?

HUGH. No.

(*There is a pause, during which* HUGH *stops pouring the drinks. Then he speaks with his back to her*)

What's his name?

LIZ (*considering whether to tell him and then knowing she's got to in the end so may as well do it now*) John Brownlow.

HUGH. How long have you known him?

LIZ. Six months.

HUGH. Where'd you meet?

LIZ. At dinner with the Chilean Ambassador.

HUGH. Was I there?

LIZ. Yes.

HUGH. Six months—March. (*He gives Liz her drink*)

LIZ. I expect so.

HUGH. Where's the Embassy?

LIZ. Don't ask me—you were driving. Somewhere by the river, I think.

HUGH. I remember. I was shouting rather loud that night. I had a row with someone in the Government about South Africa.

LIZ. That's right. We'd been to quite a lot of cocktail parties.

HUGH (*pouring his own drink*) He kept saying that my facts were wrong, which irritated me, as he'd never been there and I had—for three weeks, what's more.

LIZ. In the Game Reserve.

HUGH. He didn't know that.

LIZ. Yes, he did. I told him so at dinner.

HUGH. That's what I call loyalty.

LIZ. I didn't know that you were going to have a row with him.

HUGH. Don't tell me he's the fellow.

LIZ. No.

HUGH. He's English, is he?

LIZ. Yes.

HUGH (*moving above the card table*) More than that fellow was! That cuts the field down. Not the fellow on my right, over the coffee—he was Uruguayan. And the fellow on my left was this ass in the Government. Then opposite—round the Ambassador—were lots of diplomats. Is he a diplomat?

LIZ. No—he's a stockbroker.

HUGH (*sitting*) How old?

LIZ. Not very.

HUGH. Not compared to me! Good-looking?

LIZ. Very.

HUGH. Fair or dark?

LIZ. Fair.

HUGH. Tall or short?

LIZ. Tall.

HUGH. Spectacles?

LIZ. Yes.

(*All* LIZ's *answers can, of course, be interchangeable according to the appearance of the actor playing Brownlow*)

HUGH. Sober?

LIZ. Yes.

HUGH. I've got it—the chap in the cummerbund. What was his name again?

LIZ. John Brownlow.

HUGH. That's right—charming fellow. Said he liked my books. We dropped him at the end of Eaton Square on the way home—the Sloane Square end.

LIZ. Yes—that's right.

HUGH. Yes, of course. A very civil fellow—I remember now. What happened next?

LIZ. He rang me the next morning.

HUGH. After I'd started on the treadmill . . .

LIZ. You'd gone to Newmarket.

HUGH. What did he say?

LIZ. He asked me out to lunch.

HUGH. And you went?

LIZ. Yes.

HUGH. And it all started over sole and spinach?

LIZ. Turbot. (*She starts playing Seven Patience*)

HUGH. And he took you in a taxi to a mews off Eaton Square to help him choose a new chintz for his bedroom curtains?

LIZ. No—you've jumped the gun—he went back to the City.

HUGH. Oh—a pro! And then?

LIZ. He asked me out to dinner the next week.

HUGH. Why wasn't I there?

LIZ. You were dining with your publisher.

HUGH. And you were going with your parents to the opera.

LIZ. That's right—but Daddy got a cold.

HUGH. Your mother didn't.

LIZ. She was playing Scrabble with him.

HUGH (*watching her playing Seven Patience*) Is your mother in on this?

LIZ. Of course not—she thought I'd gone home.

HUGH. When you were choosing chintzes.

LIZ. No, I wasn't.

HUGH. Well, what were you doing?

LIZ. Dining.

HUGH. Where?

LIZ. In Charlotte Street.

HUGH. And then?

LIZ. And then he dropped me at the flat, and you came in about eleven.

HUGH. That's right. (*He rises*) Like a refill?

LIZ. No, thanks.

HUGH. I would. (*He goes over to get the drink*)

LIZ (*after a pause*) How did you find out?

HUGH. Miss Forsyth saw you in the travel agency.

LIZ. I know—I saw her. Did you put her on to me?

HUGH. Of course not—I had no idea.

LIZ. You're very unobservant. But men are.

HUGH (*moving down* C) Yes, so they tell me . . .

LIZ. Do you mean to say you've noticed nothing, all this spring and summer?

HUGH. I've been busy on my book.

LIZ. Yes, that's the trouble.

HUGH. One has got to live.

LIZ. I'm sorry.

HUGH. I did think to myself once—when I was playing golf in May—so far as I remember—that your hair was getting quite a beating-up this year. But then I got a "birdie" and forgot about it.

LIZ. What about the time you found me crying in the summer-house?

HUGH. That didn't worry me unduly.

LIZ. Well, it should have.

HUGH. I don't see why. Women cry when they're happy—like men whistle.

LIZ. In your books, I dare say.

HUGH. And in real life.

LIZ (*rising*) I don't.

HUGH. Yes, you do. You cried that time we saw the Northern Lights in Ullapool.

LIZ (*moving down* R) That was the whisky.

HUGH. Never mind—you cried.

LIZ. So you decided I'd seen the Northern Lights that evening in the summer-house in Ascot Week?

HUGH. No—I just thought you'd seen a blue-tit feeding its young —or a baby rabbit.

LIZ. Well, I hadn't.

HUGH. And you hadn't got a treble at the races?

LIZ. No.

HUGH. I'll buy it.

LIZ. I was crying because he'd asked me for the first time in the Paddock Bar. (*She sits in the armchair down* R)

HUGH (*moving upstage a pace*) Ah—the plot thickens—asked you what? (*He turns to Liz*)

LIZ. To choose his curtains.

HUGH. And what did you answer?

LIZ. Yes.

HUGH. You see—I was right. Women do cry when they're happy.

LIZ. Hugh, I wasn't happy.

HUGH. Oh, I beg your pardon.

Liz. I was miserable.

Hugh. Poor darling.

Liz. Fifteen years of faithfulness to you to end like that with one word.

Hugh. In the Paddock Bar.

Liz. We drank champagne.

Hugh. Most proper.

Liz. And he clicked his glass against mine—and his eyes were full of laughter.

Hugh. What the devil had he got to laugh about?

Liz. His latest conquest.

Hugh (*moving down* C) Oh, so he's an old campaigner—is he?

Liz. Yes—he's had three wives.

Hugh. His own—or other people's? (*He sits on the downstage sofa arm*)

Liz. Other people's first—and then his own.

Hugh. What happened to them? Thrown aside when he got tired of them?

Liz. He's a romantic.

Hugh. So that's what he is!

Liz (*rising*) It's no use trying to pretend you don't know all about him. He's well known to be the most attractive man in London.

Hugh. Greater London? Or just Mayfair?

Liz. You're being silly.

Hugh (*rising and moving above the sofa to* C) Well, you're making sweeping statements. You're talking as if you'd combed the streets round Shepherd's Bush and in the Elephant and Castle area and made comparisons. I saw a smashing speed-cop on the Chiswick over-pass last Friday for example. How does he compare with him?

Liz (*moving to the card table*) You've seen them both—make up your own mind.

Hugh (*moving down* R; *thinking it out*) Balancing the motor-bicycle against the cummerbund—That's a nice picture, isn't it?

Liz. What was Miss Forsyth doing at the travel agent's?

Hugh. Fixing up her holiday—she's off to Italy on Sunday for a fortnight—Venice, Florence, Rome—she's a Renaissance fan. Perhaps you'll meet her—you were booking on the Milan car-train, weren't you?

Liz. John was, yes—he's got business there.

Hugh. One couchette, she said.

Liz. That's right.

Hugh. Is he a very big man?

Liz. All right, you win. (*She sits on the sofa*)

Hugh. How long are you going for? (*He moves behind Liz*)

Liz. A fortnight.

Hugh. Starting when?

Liz. On Sunday morning. He's got meetings in Milan on Monday.

Hugh. For a fortnight?

LIZ. No, of course not.

HUGH. Were you going to tell me?

LIZ. Not until we were abroad.

HUGH. What were you going to tell me when you left? The hairdresser's no good on Sunday.

LIZ (*starting to play Patience again*) Mother—I was going to lunch with mother, for your benefit, at Kew. But, actually, I'm going to meet John there—and drive to Lympne—and then fly over to Le Touquet, where I would have rung you from . . .

HUGH. From where I would have rung you. (*Watching her play*) Two on three.

LIZ. Oh, yes.

HUGH. And put the King up.

LIZ. All right, I'm not blind.

HUGH. You're home now.

LIZ. No, I'm not.

HUGH (*moving above the sofa to his chair at the card table*) Bad luck. (*He watches her for a moment in silence*) Is this to be the start of the affair?

LIZ. Never you mind.

HUGH. I do mind.

LIZ. Only in so far as it might give you a good plot for your next book.

HUGH (*sitting*) One shouldn't look a gift-horse in the mouth.

LIZ. Exactly.

HUGH. And you are my wife.

LIZ. Yes, at the moment—but I won't be for long.

HUGH (*after a pause*) What does that mean?

LIZ. Just exactly what it says.

HUGH. You want a divorce.

LIZ. Yes.

HUGH. Why? Aren't you coming back after the fortnight?

LIZ. No.

HUGH. Why not?

LIZ. Because I love John.

HUGH. And you want to marry him?

LIZ. Yes, Hugh.

HUGH. And then get thrown aside when he gets tired of you?

LIZ. I'll risk that.

HUGH. I won't.

LIZ. I'm afraid you'll have to. If you won't divorce me, we'll have to live in sin, that's all.

HUGH. Put those damned cards down—put them down, I said.

(LIZ *stops playing*)

You're getting old, Liz.

LIZ. That's right.

HUGH. And I'm over fifty.

LIZ. That's right too.

HUGH. And we've got teen-age children.

LIZ. Two.

HUGH. And we both love them—and they love us.

LIZ. That's right.

HUGH. And you're going to throw all that away for one flash fellow in a cummerbund.

LIZ. He isn't flash.

HUGH. He reads that way to me.

LIZ. He's everything that you aren't.

HUGH. You'll forgive me saying so—but that's no contradiction.

LIZ. He's romantic—he's warm-blooded—he's—alive.

HUGH. It therefore follows that I'm unromantic, cold-blooded and dead.

LIZ. You said it.

HUGH. Thank you very much.

LIZ. I didn't mean it literally, darling. (*Rising and moving* C) You know just what I meant. I'm much younger than you are. Oh, I know I'm as much to blame as you are—I mean—I married you knowing that you were too old for me! But I thought I could get away with it. I can't, Hugh. I've found that out now, since I met John—I just can't.

HUGH (*persisting*) I'm sorry to be so persistent, but is this to be the start of the affair—this couchette on the Milan train—or have the tapes gone up already?

LIZ. Why should I tell you?

HUGH. Because I'd like to know how far the rot's set in.

LIZ (*moving down* R) I'm going to marry him, Hugh—that's how far it's set in.

HUGH (*after a pause*) When was Ascot?

LIZ. June, some time.

HUGH. The third week—that's right. (*Rising*) And it's the third week in July now. A month in fact, since you said "Yes". And you're in love with him. What's more, you're quite prepared to go to Milan without telling me—except when it's too late. (*Moving to the drinks table*) Now, let me see—if I was working out a plot like that, with characters behaving like that, I'd reckon they'd be in it right over their gumboots. Right?

LIZ (*circling the armchair down* R) You're always right, Hugh—aren't you—when it comes to sex. That's what the critics all agree about whatever else they may say—"Mr Walford, with his quite uncanny 'insight' into every woman's heart leads us enchantingly . . ."

HUGH (*interrupting*) What sort of curtains are they?

LIZ. Bright red velvet.

HUGH (*moving down* C) And you chose them the week-end that I was fishing down in Stockbridge and you went allegedly to the Palladium with your old nanny.

LIZ. Yes. I rang her up—and said I had 'flu, so she took her sister.

HUGH. And you hung them the next week-end when you went

allegedly to stay with Mabel Stourton down in Kent after her nervous breakdown.

LIZ. That's right. I invented all that—Mabel never had a nervous breakdown. She was playing golf at Rye that week-end, and she won the competition, what's more.

HUGH. Good for her.

LIZ (*sitting down* R) I was afraid you might have seen it in *The Times*.

HUGH. I did.

LIZ. You did!

HUGH. That's what I said.

LIZ. But weren't you surprised?

HUGH. No.

LIZ. No! A woman with a nervous breakdown winning six and five!

HUGH. She played extremely well—I went and watched her.

LIZ. Watched her!

HUGH. From a decent distance. She did one chip straight from Heaven, landed full pitch in the hole—an "eagle".

LIZ. So you've known the whole time?

HUGH (*moving* LC) Yes.

LIZ. Since when?

HUGH. Since Mrs Chilean Ambassador said "Do you know John Brownlow" and you said "No"—and shook hands. Your eyes were dancing like a pair of stars.

LIZ. You were behind me.

HUGH (*moving to the sofa and sitting*) They were dancing all the evening like they used to when we were engaged. And every time I tried to walk between you after dinner in the drawing-room to the drinks table, I had to break some sort of barrier.

LIZ. What nonsense!

HUGH. No, I did. Some kind of ray—like burglars do in banks—and alarm bells were ringing everywhere—and police cars dashing by—and sirens hooting—every portent you could want, in fact, except a thunderstorm.

LIZ (*rising and moving* C) Why didn't you say anything?

HUGH. I did—I quarrelled with that bloody Under-Secretary about South Africa.

LIZ. But then you offered John a lift, when we left.

HUGH. Why not? It was raining and he hadn't got a coat.

LIZ. But, if you knew . . .

HUGH. I should have let him get pneumonia.

LIZ (*moving above the sofa to the fire*) You should have said something. You might have stopped it in time.

HUGH. It was too late when it started.

LIZ. No.

HUGH. Yes—nothing would have stopped it.

LIZ. If you'd taken me away . . .

HUGH. Where to?

LIZ. The South of France—or Spain—Marbella . . . (*pronounced* "*Marbeya*").

HUGH (*rising and moving to the drinks table*) Wouldn't have done any good. It would have made it worse in fact. You would have seen the fellow sitting with you every night at dinner—fondling his brandy at the table—sitting in the lounge behind a big cigar and swotting up *The Times* when you went up to bed—having a night-cap on the terrace in his dressing-gown—watching the moonlight on the sea—then turning round and turning into me. It would have made it worse.

LIZ. It couldn't be worse than it is now.

HUGH. Poor old girl—you've got it badly haven't you?

LIZ. You make it sound like measles!

HUGH (*moving to Liz*) Let me top it up for you.

LIZ (*giving him her glass*) All right.

HUGH (*going to refill both glasses*) Well, it was bound to happen in the end.

LIZ. Why?

HUGH. Why? Old Mother Nature! Look at red deer. Every old stag looks up from the heather one fine day—and sees a pair of antlers on the sky-line—then a pair of ears—and then a handsome head and thick set neck—and then a glossy body, rippling with muscle—and he knows he's had it . . .

LIZ. Not without a fight.

HUGH (*giving Liz her drink*) Oh yes, he fights all right. But he's an animal. (*He fetches his own drink*) He didn't go to Eton. But it doesn't do him any damned good—just prolongs the agony and makes the hind just that much keener on the other fellow—most unwise. Imagine me and Brownlow with our antlers locked together, roaring round and round the drawing-room at the Chilean Ambassador's, with you up on the piano with your nostrils quivering—and your ears flapping to keep off the flies. It wouldn't make a very pretty picture, would it? Let's be civilized at least—and take defeat with dignity.

LIZ. So you accept defeat?

HUGH. Of course I do. It had to happen as I say. The only questions were "when" and "in what form". Now we've had the answer to both questions and we've got to make the best of it. Damn funny! Fifteen years of marriage—then it happens, just like that! One moment you're going upstairs, married to the eyebrows—solid as the Bank of England. The next, you're split right down the middle like a ruddy atom—back where you were in your twenties—all alone and screaming for your mother.

LIZ. Speak for yourself.

HUGH (*moving down* R) That's exactly what I'm doing. (*He sits down* R) Do you know, I damned near took that butler's hand and went out of the room in tears. Instead, I swallowed four Martinis in as many minutes—much more sensible at my age—and much more constructive. Why don't stockbrokers commute instead of dining out with South American Ambassadors?

Liz. He stays in London during the week.

Hugh (*after a pause*) What about the children.

Liz. His? Or ours?

Hugh. Ours.

Liz. What about them?

Hugh. Were you going to tell them?

Liz. No—I thought it'd come much better from you—as you were the injured party.

Hugh. You mean that you funked it?

Liz. Naturally, I didn't want to even see them till I'd made the final break and it was too late to go back on it.

Hugh. What if I pick that telephone up now—and get them back from school?

Liz. You wouldn't do that, would you?

Hugh (*rising and moving to the desk*) No—I'm not that bitter.

Liz (*sitting on the chair at the card table*) You'll get their custody, of course, but I hope you'll let them come and stay with John and me when we're married.

Hugh. In the Mews flat?

Liz. No—in Gloucestershire. He's got a country house there.

Hugh. Big or small?

Liz. Quite big enough.

Hugh. What acreage?

Liz (*with a shrug*) Five hundred.

Hugh. Farm? (*He moves to the sofa*)

Liz. Yes.

Hugh. Well to do, then.

Liz. Comfortable.

Hugh. In spite of alimony three times over.

Liz. He gets by. Sheila and Dick'll like him.

Hugh. Good.

Liz. He's very good with children.

Hugh (*sitting on the upstage arm of the sofa*) Other people's? Or his own?

Liz. Both.

Hugh. What's he chalked up so far?

Liz. Three—one by each wife.

Hugh. Boys or girls?

Liz. Both.

Hugh. Hermaphrodites?

Liz. Two boys—one girl.

Hugh. Living with him?

Liz. No—with their mothers.

Hugh. So you'll be alone.

Liz. Yes.

Hugh. Strolling round the park, knee deep in bluebells.

LIZ. Bluebells don't grow knee-high.
HUGH. Brussels-sprouts then . . .
LIZ. Ha! Ha!
HUGH. It's all physical you know.
LIZ. Yes—at the moment—anyway.
HUGH. It always will be.
LIZ. No.
HUGH. Yes, darling.
LIZ. You're jealous.
HUGH. Naturally, but that's not why I'm saying it. I'm saying it because you wouldn't want to leave me if it weren't . . .
LIZ. Wouldn't I?
HUGH. No. As a lover, I may be inadequate, I'll grant you that—
LIZ. That's big of you!
HUGH. —but, every other way, I'm what the doctor ordered—kind, amusing, unpredictable in conversation and behaviour, interesting, well-read and generous.
LIZ. That's not enough—not for a woman.
HUGH. You've been satisfied for fifteen years.
LIZ. No, Hugh, I haven't.
HUGH. You've been happy.
LIZ. Negatively.
HUGH. Nonsense.
LIZ. It's not nonsense, Hugh—it's true. (*Rising and moving above the sofa to* c) Oh, I've been happy, but I haven't been alive. If vegetables are happy, I've been happy—but that's all.
HUGH. You've hidden it well.
LIZ. Thank you.
HUGH. You were happy when we married.
LIZ. Yes.
HUGH. And on our honeymoon.
LIZ. Yes—at the start. (*Moving down* R) And then I started Sheila—and that was a different thing—and then I started Dick—and so was that. And then I had to bring them up and that was new and satisfying and exciting. But now that's all over—they've grown up.
HUGH. Not quite.
LIZ. Well, very nearly. And now there's just you and me.
HUGH. And I lack glamour.
LIZ. If you put it like that—yes.
HUGH. And Brownlow doesn't.
LIZ. No. (*Moving to the sofa*) Don't think I'm blaming you—I'm not. It's just the way things go. You're older than me—much much older. And it's not surprising that you've reached the age when you don't want or need the things that I do.
HUGH (*after a pause*) So it's physical, as I said. (*He rises to the fireplace*)
LIZ. All right then, it is.

HUGH. It won't last.

LIZ. I'm afraid I disagree.

HUGH. It didn't with the other ones.

LIZ. They weren't up to it.

HUGH. Maybe they got bored.

LIZ (*moving down* R) Nonsense—they're all in love with him still.

HUGH. Have they signed an affidavit?

LIZ. It's quite obvious.

HUGH. You've met them, have you?

LIZ. No. I've seen their letters though.

HUGH. They all keep up their correspondence, do they?

LIZ. Yes—they're all great friends still.

HUGH (*moving down* C; *with the first note of bitterness in his voice*) Pity that he's not a Moslem.

(*There is a pause. A train is heard in the distance*)

LIZ (*moving down* C) I'm so sorry.

HUGH. That's all right.

LIZ. We'll always be friends, won't we, Hugh? Like John is with his exes. It's the only civilized way of behaving. And it won't upset the children. They'll be able to respect us both still. And do half the holidays with each of us.

HUGH. Not these next holidays, I hope.

LIZ. No, after the divorce is through, I mean.

HUGH (*moving to the desk*) Mrs John Brownlow the Fourth!

LIZ. No need—all the exes married again.

HUGH. Well done them. (*He pauses*) Where's Brownlow now?

LIZ. In London.

HUGH. In the Mews flat?

LIZ. I imagine so.

HUGH. Poor devil—on a Friday night in London. Ring him up and ask him down here. Go on. Does he play golf?

LIZ. Yes, I think so.

HUGH. Well then, I'll have a round tomorrow morning with him —if he'd like to. Then he can come on to lunch and stay till you push off on Sunday morning. What's the number? I'll do it, if you're shy.

LIZ (*moving* L *of the desk*) Don't be ridiculous—it's quite out of the question.

HUGH. Why—it'll clear the air. I'm sure he hates this hole and corner stuff as much as you do. Anyway, I'd like to vet him. Otherwise, I'd always feel I hadn't been responsible.

LIZ. You may not like him.

HUGH. 'Course I will, dear. "Any friend of yours etc." What's the number? (*He lifts the receiver*)

LIZ. I'll do it upstairs from my bedroom. (*She takes the receiver from him*)

HUGH. All right, but he'll be asleep soon—the poor fellow!

LIZ. I'm just going up. (*She replaces the receiver*)

HUGH. Good. You look tired, dear—I should take some Metatone to Italy if I were you. I'll get some on my way down to the Club House in the morning.

LIZ. Thank you. Well, I'll say good night.

HUGH. Good night, Liz.

LIZ. Good night, Hugh. (*She moves to the door up* LC)

HUGH. Tell him to meet me at the Club House between half-past ten and quarter to eleven. We'll play a dozen holes and then be back around a quarter to one. What's his handicap?

LIZ. Don't ask me.

HUGH. Never mind, dear. (*Moving down* R) I will.

LIZ (*turning at the door*) It won't make you any happier, Hugh.

HUGH. What won't?

LIZ. Asking him down.

HUGH. I'll get some exercise though. (*He sits down* R)

LIZ (*moving down* C) You'll be punishing yourself that's all. It won't do any good. And it'll merely be embarrassing for all of us.

HUGH. I can't see why. If I'm prepared to go through with it, there's no reason why you two should funk it. I'm the only loser, after all. Besides, the whole affair wants talking over.

LIZ. Talking over?

HUGH. The divorce, I mean. Who's going to cite who—and so on, and so forth.

LIZ. You're going to cite John naturally.

HUGH. No, on the contrary. I'd like to give you a divorce.

LIZ. That's too old-fashioned for words, darling.

HUGH. Maybe so. But that's the way it's going to be.

LIZ. You mean that you'll go to Brighton with some blonde?

HUGH. No, darling—I won't go to Brighton—and the blonde'll come to me.

LIZ. Here!

HUGH. Yes—why not?

LIZ. But what will Mrs Gray say?

HUGH. Quite a lot, in Court—I hope! About what she saw when she brought the breakfast in—"The Master, he was sitting up in bed, my lord, with one arm round the lady and the other, roving like. And when I says 'Good morning', he says, 'Make a note of it, then, Mrs Gray.' " And, as I don't defend it, you can marry John as soon as it's made absolute.

LIZ. You're very generous, Hugh.

HUGH. It's the least that I can do for you, my dear.

LIZ. Who will you choose? A lady from some strip-club?

HUGH. No. Why ask a stranger—when it's possible to ask a friend.

LIZ. Who have you got in mind—the Vicar's wife?

HUGH. Miss Forsyth, probably.

LIZ. Miss Forsyth! Don't be silly—she's your secretary.

HUGH. Maybe she is—but she's most faithful. And she's been in love with me for years.

Liz. Well, if you're determined to talk nonsense, I'll say "good night". *(She moves to the door)*

Hugh. Liz.

Liz *(turning)* Yes, Hugh?

Hugh. What's this fellow Brownlow got that I've not got? In one word—or two—if you find it more convenient.

Liz. Good night *(She moves towards the door again)*

Hugh. No, I want to know, Liz. I'm not joking.

Liz. That's a nice change.

Hugh. Come on, darling. Out with it. Cards on the table—please —I want to know.

Liz *(moving down c)* He treats me like a man should treat a woman.

Hugh. Cave-man stuff, you mean.

Liz. You know exactly what I mean, Hugh.

Hugh. And he flatters you as well, I bet.

Liz. He tells me that I'm beautiful, if that's what you mean. He appreciates me.

Hugh. And I don't.

Liz. One wouldn't notice it.

Hugh. Don't be a damned fool, Liz. Of course you're beautiful— you always have been.

Liz. Women like to be reminded of those sort of things.

Hugh. I can't see why. You've got a mirror, haven't you?

Liz. It doesn't talk, Hugh.

Hugh. I'd have thought it did, in your case.

Liz. Well, it doesn't say the right things.

Hugh. Unlike Brownlow.

(Liz *moves to the card table*)

Yes. I see it all now. *(He rises and moves to the drinks table)* Cave man Brownlow in skins with a club in one hand and a carrot in the other, taking you away from me in my old Jaeger dressing-gown and carpet slippers. Technique—that's it, isn't it—technique. I've always lacked it. Maybe I'm too sensitive—or too insensitive. Or maybe I'm just lazy. *(He refills his glass)* Don't let me detain you, darling—I'm just thinking aloud.

(Liz *moves to the door, then turns back*)

Or maybe I'm just queer. That's a good thought, isn't it? Sailing for half a century under a false flag!

(Liz *smiles at this, but* Hugh *does not see it as his back is still turned*)

(Facing her) One for the stairs?

Liz. All right, but just a drop.

Hugh *(pouring a drink for her)* Do you think that's the answer? If it is, I must confess that everything drops into place at once. The fact that I'm so popular with women readers—and the fact that I'm reacting to the break-up of my marriage like this. I'm an ineffectual old queer whose life's entirely centred round himself and his romantic novels. I don't give a damn for you, or Brownlow, or divorce, or Dick, or Sheila. All I care about is continuity and comfort. I'm a hedonist, in fact, my darling. Quite a good word, isn't it? (*He hands her the drink*)

Liz. What does it mean?

Hugh. A pleasure-lover—a narcissist. Someone who sees everything, including marriage, in relation to himself. And Brownlow's just the opposite, I should imagine—thinking only of you. I'll bet he concentrates like no one's business. You needn't tell me if you'd rather not.

Liz (*moving down* C) That's most broadminded of you.

Hugh. I once knew a don at Oxford who couldn't understand all the fuss about sex, as he said it only took place about three times a year at the outside. I wouldn't wholly subscribe to that view, but I can see what he meant. Maybe men are like steaks—rare, medium or overdone. If so, I know which I am.

Liz. I'll second that.

Hugh. I'm sorry—obviously I've been most inadequate. (*He moves to the card table*) And you've been very noble, putting up with it for so long. But as I've already said, the break was bound to come one day. So run along, my darling, now—and ring the fellow up.

Liz. You're sure you want him, Hugh?

Hugh (*moving to Liz down* C) Yes, naturally I want to meet the fellow. I've got a proprietary interest in you, after all, my dear. Like handing one's tank over in the last war to another squadron officer. I'll turn the lights out.

Liz. Thank you. If I'd known that you were going to take it like this, I'd have told you earlier. I hated all the deceit.

Hugh. Never mind that—everything's all right now.

Liz. Good night, Hugh.

(Liz *kisses Hugh, gives him her glass, and exits*)

Hugh. Good night, Liz . . . (*He puts the glasses on the table and turns off the lights up* LC. *Then he goes to turn off the desk lamp*)

(*The telephone tinkles a little, as* Liz *makes her call from upstairs.* Hugh *looks at the instrument, then up at the ceiling, then picks up the receiver*)

Hugh (*at the telephone*) Hullo—sorry to butt in, Liz, but I'd like to ask the fellow something. Brownlow, are you there? . . . Oh, good. I'm Liz's husband, Hugh. She's told you about golf tomorrow morning, has she? . . . And is it all right? Oh, good—that's first class. I was wondering if you'd have time to call at Harrods and pick up an eight-ounce jar of caviare on your way down . . . You would? Good man. And put it down to me—Hugh—well you know the other name by now, I shouldn't wonder! . . . Good, well, see you at the Golf Club between half-past ten and quarter-to-eleven. You can't miss it.

There's a great big sign up, saying "Stonewall Golf Course" with an arrow pointing in the right direction more or less. Well, I'll look forward to it. We've a lot to talk about I gather. Well, good night, so sorry to butt in. All yours, my darling. (*He is about to put the receiver down and then picks it up again*) By the way, what handicap do you play off? . . . Hullo, hullo, what's happened to the fellow, Liz? . . . Oh, why did he do that, I wonder? . . . You keep saying that, but why? Why should he be embarrassed—if I'm not? Yes, all right, darling—leave the water in for me—I'll be up quite soon. Sleep well. (*He hangs up, stands thinking for a while, with his drink, and then goes back to the telephone and dials*) Miss Forsyth? Mr Walford here . . . Oh, good—not asleep, I hope? . . . Oh, I'm so sorry. I won't be a second and then you can get back to the programme. Could you catch the train tomorrow morning that arrives here at twelve-twenty? . . . You could—good—well, I'll be playing golf, and we'll pick you up on our way home for lunch. (*He is about to put it down when he adds an afterthought*) And bring your sleeping-bag—we may be working late.

HUGH *replaces the receiver, as—*

the CURTAIN *falls*

SCENE 2

SCENE—*The same. Saturday morning, between half-past twelve and one.*
When the CURTAIN *rises,* LIZ *is finishing off the flowers, standing at the table*
R *which has now been moved further into the room. She has done the drawing-room flowers, those she is doing now are for the bedrooms. The card-table and chair have been removed, and the sofa and table turned to face more directly downstage. The stool has also been removed from* RC. MRS GRAY *enters with an ice bucket, which she puts on the drinks table.*

LIZ. Oh thank you, Mrs Gray—I could have done that.
MRS GRAY. Don't you worry, dear. You've other things to think about, poor lamb.
LIZ. What an extraordinary remark to make.
MRS GRAY. Well, it's made now—and I feel better for it.

(LIZ *starts for the door with two small vases of flowers*)

Let me take those.
LIZ. I can manage.
MRS GRAY. No—no—you've your guests to think about, dear. And there's nothing doing in the kitchen at the moment, with the first course being caviare—according to what Mr Walford said.
LIZ. Oh, well—it's very sweet of you . . .
MRS GRAY. No trouble at all, dearie.

LIZ. That one's for Miss Forsyth in the spare room. And that one's for Mr Brownlow in the spare room dressing-room.

MRS GRAY. But he's in Mr Walford's dressing-room, Ma'am.

LIZ. Who is?

MRS GRAY. Mr Brownlow.

LIZ. Really, Mrs Gray—who said so?

MRS GRAY. Mr Walford, Ma'am—as he was going off for golf. "Put Mr Brownlow in my dressing-room", he says, "And move my things into the spare room dressing-room."

LIZ. Mr Walford said that?

MRS GRAY. Yes. And when I said—"Well, that's a funny thing", he said, "Wait till you see Miss Forsyth, Mrs Gray, and you won't think so." Then he winked at me.

LIZ (*moving below the sofa to down L*) And have you moved his things?

MRS GRAY (*putting the vases on the drinks table*) Yes, and it's taken me all morning.

(LIZ *decides not to ask her to move them back, and lights a cigarette*)

I'm sorry for you dear—I really am. (*Moving down C*) All these years looking after him—and bringing up the children—and he brings a bit down here, as bold as brass and cracking jokes about it.

LIZ. She's his secretary, Mrs Gray.

MRS GRAY. That's what he told me, but it doesn't make it any better.

LIZ (*moving C*) You know Mr Walford by now, surely Mrs Gray, and he was joking, as you say.

MRS GRAY. That's what I thought at first. But when I thought it over afterwards, when I was hoovering—I didn't think so. Not after that wink. I've seen men wink like that before and I don't like it. You know—trying to get round you, like a naughty schoolboy who's been stealing apples. Still, as he's a writer, I suppose you have to make allowances, but in his own . . .

LIZ (*moving down R*) That's just it, that's the explanation. He's right in the middle of a book now, and Miss Forsyth types them all for him. And sometimes he gets inspiration in the night—and so—to save disturbing me—and everything . . . (*She finishes lamely*)

MRS GRAY. You'll go to Heaven—you will, bless you! (*She moves up C*)

LIZ. Well, I'm sure we'll meet there, Mrs Gray.

MRS GRAY. I hope so, anyway—I've done my best. (*She goes to pick up the vases*) I'll tell you something, dear. When Mr Gray tried it on once with me, I hit him with a bottle—well, you've seen the scar, dear—his war wound, he calls it—and the best name for it too.

(*There is the sound of two cars arriving*)

LIZ (*moving to the door*) I'll open the door for you.

Mrs Gray. Thank you. Like a brand it is, I always tell him—like they put on cattle in the Argentine or Texas on the tele. Every time he has a shave, he sees it in the mirror and he knows who he belongs to. Here's the car, dear. (*She moves to the window*)

Liz. Yes, well, run along.

Mrs Gray (*trying to linger*) It's this one for Miss Forsyth and this one for Mr Brownlow. There's another car.

Liz. That's Mr Brownlow's—he drove down from London.

Mrs Gray. And there's no flowers for the Master?

Liz. No.

Mrs Gray (*still lingering*) And quite right, too. (*She moves to the door*) I call it a shame, I do. (*She moves back to Liz*) What's this Mr Brownlow like?

Liz (*pushing her out gently*) He's very nice.

Mrs Gray. Well, you get off with him, dear. That's the ticket. Make him jealous and see how he likes it.

Liz. Run along, please, Mrs Gray, or they'll think I forgot to do the flowers.

(Mrs Gray *exits.* Liz *shuts the door behind her and moves to the sofa table*)

Hugh (*off*) Well in you go, Miss Forsyth. Mind the step. We don't want you arriving on all fours.

(Hugh *enters through the french windows with* Miss Forsyth, *who moves* RC. *She is younger than Liz, and very good-looking*)

Let's see, Liz, you don't know Miss Forsyth, do you? (*He returns to the windows for John*)

Miss Forsyth. Hello, Mrs Walford.

Liz (*shaking hands*) I do hope you had a good trip down.

Miss Forsyth. Yes, thank you. (*She moves upstage a little*)

Hugh (*to John*) Mind the step.

(John Brownlow *enters through the windows. He also is good-looking, and not unduly flash*)

And I think you two know each other? (*He does an introductory gesture with his hands*)

Liz. Hullo, John.

John. Hullo, Liz.

Hugh (*coming forward to Liz* C *with a couple of parcels in his hands*) Here's your Metatone, my darling. Give it to Miss Forsyth, otherwise you're certain to forget it. To be packed, Miss Forsyth. Mrs Walford's off to Italy tomorrow morning. Pack it with a tea-spoon in the square red jewel case, wouldn't you think, darling?

Liz. I should think so.

Hugh. And then you can get your hands on it, whenever you feel like a swig. At Domodossola—or in the Great St Bernard Tunnel, if you go that way.

Liz. Yes, thank you, Hugh.

Hugh. And here's the caviare that Brownlow very kindly brought down with him.

Liz (*seizing this excuse to retire*) Oh yes—I'll take it in to Mrs Gray.

(*She moves to the door up* LC *and exits*)

Hugh (*as Liz goes*) Don't let her have too much—it's wasted on her.

(*By now* Liz *has gone, ignoring this, so* Hugh *turns to Brownlow*)

Mrs Gray's our house-keeper-cook-charlady combined—and Gray's our gardener. Now, you two haven't met before, I take it.

John. No, I think not.

Hugh. Well, Miss Forsyth is my secretary, Brownlow.

John. Ah, yes.

Hugh (*to Miss Forsyth*) And my wife was telling me last night that Mr Brownlow is the most attractive man in London.

John. Nonsense. (*He moves down* R)

Hugh. Not to speak of the most modest. (*He moves to the drinks table*) Now then who'd like a drink? Miss Forsyth?

Miss Forsyth. Thank you, Mr Walford. (*She moves above the sofa to the fire*)

Hugh. Gin and tonic? Sherry? Gin and bitter lemon?

Miss Forsyth. Sherry please.

Hugh. You, Brownlow?

John. Could I have a gin and tonic, Walford?

Hugh. Why not? I'll join you. Thirsty work in those damned bunkers. I know what a camel feels like in a sand-storm now. Now, let me see, have you been here before, Miss Forsyth?

Miss Forsyth. No.

Hugh (*moving to Miss Forsyth and handing her a glass of sherry*) Well, we must make the most of it.

(Liz *enters, overhearing this remark*)

(*Moving to the drinks table*) Ah, there you are. What are you drinking, darling?

Liz. I think I'll have a glass of sherry. Don't you bother, I'll do it. (*She pours herself a sherry*)

Hugh. Do you like ice, Brownlow?

John. Yes, please.

Hugh. Is there any?

Liz. Yes, of course there is.

Hugh (*cheerfully*) I say—what a surprise! And a slice of lemon?

John. Thank you.

Hugh. Dead on time, Miss Forsyth's train was, darling.

Liz. Oh. Good.

Hugh. Hadn't been there half a minute when it came in and we saw Miss Forsyth tripping down the platform looking like a lovely flower—a passion flower to be precise.

MISS FORSYTH. You're being silly, Mr Walford. (*She sits on the sofa*)

HUGH. On the contrary, I'm being accurate. (*To John*) Your drink. You read "Maud" don't you, Brownlow?

JOHN. Maud?

HUGH. "Maud" Tennyson. Let's see—how does it go? Ah yes— (*He quotes at Miss Forsyth*)
"There has fallen a splendid tear from
   the passion-flower at the gate.
She is coming, my dove, my dear—she
   is coming my love, my fate
And the red rose cries . . ."

(HUGH *pauses to try and remember how it goes on and* LIZ *takes the opportunity to interrupt him*)

LIZ. Who won your golf?

HUGH (*surrendering and going back to mix his own drink*) Need you ask, darling?

LIZ. You, John?

JOHN. Well, yes—actually I did.

HUGH. I never had a hope.

JOHN. Don't listen to him. I was flat out.

HUGH. Were you, old chap? Well, you didn't show it—that's all I can say. We only played nine holes because we had to meet Miss Forsyth's train and he won five and four.

LIZ. Well done, John. (*She moves to the sofa and sits* R)

HUGH. On a strange course, too. Technique, that's what I told him in the Club House, wasn't it? Technique. (*Moving down* C) The fellow who's got better technique than the other fellow always wins, whatever game it is, and whatever the handicap. Well, good luck all.

MISS FORSYTH. Good luck.

JOHN. Cheers.

LIZ. Good luck.

HUGH (*to John*) Taking your clubs with you on the Milan train?

JOHN. Well, yes—I thought I would.

HUGH (*to Liz*) You'd better take yours, darling. Make a note of it, Miss Forsyth. Metatone and golf-clubs. Mrs Walford's going on a holiday with Mr Brownlow, leaving in the morning. Well, you knew that, didn't you?

MISS FORSYTH. Well, yes, I did.

HUGH (*to John*) She saw you in the travel agency.

JOHN. Oh, really.

HUGH. Yes—on Thursday—booking the couchette—more ice?

JOHN. No, thank you.

HUGH. You, Miss Forsyth? (*He moves above the sofa*)

MISS FORSYTH. Well, just half a glass.

HUGH (*taking Miss Forsyth's glass to the drinks table*) And she put one

and one together and decided that it made two. So she came and told
me, like the loyal girl she is.

MISS FORSYTH. It sounds too interfering for words put like that.

HUGH. What nonsense. It was most efficient. Mr Brownlow and
my wife are going to run away, Miss Forsyth.

MISS FORSYTH. Oh dear—I'm so sorry.

HUGH. Don't be—they're in love with one another.

JOHN (*moving up* RC) Really, Walford!

HUGH. And I'm giving my wife a divorce and then they'll get
married.

LIZ. Really darling—you're being too embarrassing for words.

HUGH (*coming back with a glass in each hand*) I can't see why. It's
only civil to put Miss— Good Heavens, anyone'd think that we were
in the office—what's your Christian name again, dear?

MISS FORSYTH. Molly.

HUGH. That's right—well done. May I call you Molly, as we're on
holiday?

MISS FORSYTH. Of course.

HUGH (*handing Molly her glass*) Your sherry, Molly.

MOLLY. Thank you, Mr Walford.

HUGH. Hugh's the name.

MOLLY. Hugh.

HUGH. Gin and tonic, John?

JOHN. No thank you, Walford.

HUGH. Hugh's the name still.

JOHN. No thanks, Hugh. (*He moves down* R)

HUGH. Good! That's it. That's the ticket. (*Moving above the sofa to
Liz*) Now we're all friends. No more tension. (*He slaps Liz on the
shoulder*) No more thunderclouds. The cumuli have broken up—the
sun's come through—the birds are singing. And I want a spot more
gin-and-tonic! What about you, darling?

LIZ. I'm all right, thanks.

HUGH. Well, I'll take your word for it—what time's lunch?

LIZ. One.

HUGH (*looking at his watch*) Good—time to see the garden. How
about a walk round, Molly—with your sherry?

MOLLY. I'd love to.

HUGH. Good girl. (*Moving* RC *to John*) Liz is a great gardener.
She's got green fingers. I'm just the destroyer—passion-flowers and
bind-weed—ivy and delphiniums—they all fall to my axe. Do you
have window-boxes in your flat, John?

JOHN. Yes.

HUGH. What do you grow in them?

JOHN. Geraniums.

HUGH. Did Liz plant them?

JOHN. Yes.

HUGH. Oh well—you're all right. I'll bet they're climbing round
the bath-taps now! Ready, Molly? (*He moves up* C)

MOLLY (*getting up*) Yes—indeed.

(MOLLY *moves above the sofa*)

HUGH. Right. Through the door the way you came in. Mind the step—it may be trickier than when you came in—with the sherry. Coming, John?

(MOLLY *exits to the garden*)

JOHN. I'll stay here if you don't mind.

HUGH. Not a bit, old fellow, not a bit. And help yourself if you feel thirsty. All right, darling?

LIZ. Yes, of course I'm all right.

HUGH. Good. Well, have another glass of sherry and relax yourself. You look a bit strung up. (*To John*) She's pretty, don't you think?

JOHN. Of course I do.

HUGH. No, I mean Molly. (*Moving* R *to John and leaning confidentially to prevent Molly hearing*) Hot stuff too, they tell me. At least, that was the *on dit* when she worked in my publisher's office. And she's got a passion for me. Funny, isn't it—considering I'm old enough to be her father. Still, one never knows with women—they're rum things.

LIZ. You're being very rude, Hugh.

HUGH. Rude, dear—why—I like rum—Oh, I see—yes—sorry. Coming, Molly.

(HUGH *nips out to the garden*)

(*Off*) Sorry, dear—let's start on the herbaceous border first . . .

LIZ. It's too pathetic, isn't it?

JOHN (*moving to the drinks table*) And damned embarrassing.

LIZ (*rising and moving down* R) Do you know that he's put you in his dressing-room? (*She puts her drink on the table*)

JOHN. Good God!

LIZ (*picking up the waste-paper basket and putting in the wrapping and pieces from the flowers*) And himself in the spare-room dressing-room next to Miss Forsyth.

JOHN (*moving to the desk with the basket*) That's just bluff—don't let it worry you.

LIZ (*returning* R *for her glass*) It doesn't worry me. It worries Mrs Gray, though. It'll be all round the village by this evening.

JOHN. Well, it will be by tomorrow evening anyway.

LIZ. She thinks that she's his mistress. She came in and tried to mother me this morning just before you got here. Called me "dearie" and "poor lamb".

JOHN (*moving to the sofa*) She doesn't know about us, then?

LIZ. Of course not.

JOHN (*sitting on the sofa*) I thought that your husband might have told her in that charming open way he has.

LIZ (*moving* R *of the sofa*) Why did you come down, John?
JOHN. You told me to.
LIZ. I know—I thought I couldn't stand it by myself until tomorrow, once I knew he'd found out.
JOHN (*rising*) My poor darling. Did you have a dreadful night?
LIZ (*crossing below John and moving down* L) I never slept a wink.
JOHN. It evidently suits you. You're looking wonderful.
LIZ. I'm not, John.
JOHN (*gently*) Yes, you are. (*Moving to Liz*) Have some more sherry?
LIZ. No, thanks. Was the golf a nightmare?
JOHN. Not too bad.
LIZ. Were you on time?
JOHN. Yes.
LIZ. What did Hugh say when you met?
JOHN. "Good morning—I'm Hugh Walford."
LIZ. What did you say?
JOHN. "I'm John Brownlow."
LIZ. Is that all?
JOHN. It seemed to cover everything. Well, most things, anyway.
(*He sits on the sofa*)
LIZ. And then?
JOHN. We went inside and paid our green fees. At least, he did.
LIZ. You let him pay yours?
JOHN. He wouldn't hear of anything else.
LIZ. And you really beat him, five and four?
JOHN. Yes.
LIZ. Was he very bad?
JOHN. He did some good shots—but they weren't very straight.
LIZ (*moving above the sofa to* RC) And yours were?
JOHN. Straighter—and he found a lot of bunkers.
LIZ. And you didn't?
JOHN. I was lucky.
LIZ. Poor Hugh.
JOHN. Now, don't start getting sentimental.
LIZ. But he's so good usually.
JOHN. I dare say—but I'm better.
LIZ. Yes, of course you are. And did he talk about us?
JOHN. Not a word.
LIZ. Not even in the car?
JOHN. We were in different cars.
LIZ. Well, in the Club House?
JOHN. No.
LIZ. Aren't men extraordinary!
JOHN. Some men, I dare say.
LIZ. You're just as bad. You should have talked to him.
JOHN. I did.
LIZ. About us?

JOHN. No.

LIZ. Why not?

JOHN. Well, what is there to say, for God's sake?

LIZ. Quite a lot, I should have thought.

JOHN. Not anything he doesn't know already.

LIZ. I just think you ought to tell him that you love me.

JOHN. Darling, that goes without saying.

LIZ. Oh, does it?

JOHN. Yes, of course it does. (*Rising and moving down* C) No, if we're going to have a "man to man" together, it'll be about the damn fool way that he's behaving.

LIZ. Don't be hard on him. He's never grown up.

JOHN. Well, it's time he did.

LIZ. Perhaps, but you do like him, don't you?

JOHN. Yes—he's charming. But I like you better. Put that glass down. Put it down, I said. Now, come . . .

(LIZ *puts her glass on the table* R)

Now come here. (*He kisses her*) Darling.

(HUGH *comes in* R *and watches them embracing*)

(*Breaking the embrace and looking into her eyes*) Liz, my darling.

LIZ. Johnski—oh, my darling Johnski.

(LIZ *and* JOHN *kiss.* HUGH *moves down and taps Liz on the shoulder.* LIZ *moves down* R, JOHN *to* LC)

HUGH. Hold it just a second—if you don't mind. Sorry, old chap, didn't mean to butt in, but it's Molly. She's got bogged down on the croquet lawn in her high heels. (*To Liz*) Have you got a pair of sandals handy?

LIZ. There're some in the flower-room. I'll get them.

HUGH. Thank you, darling.

(LIZ *exits* R)

(*To John*) There's a touch of lip-stick on your left cheek.

(JOHN *takes out a handkerchief and dabs at his right cheek*)

Left, I said—old chap—

(JOHN *gets the right spot, then sits* L *on the sofa*)

That's better. (*He strolls to the table up* L, *picks up two photographs and moves down* L) Really puts her back into it, old Liz, doesn't she? She damn near broke my neck the first time that I met her. In a Land Rover, it was—in Scotland, north of Carlisle somewhere—we'd been out fishing and I stopped to light a cigarette and she was on me like a panther. Everything went—matches—cigarette-case and the button on my shirt collar. I reckon I was lucky not to finish up in hospital. Still, it was worth it. (*He gives John the photographs*) This is Dick—and this is Sheila. You'll be seeing quite a lot of them in future, I imagine. Sheila's very like her mother—goes right off the deep-end. She'll be a push-over for any over-sexed young bounder in jeans. Dick's more like me—full of charm but just about as lively as a tortoise. I expect he'll write books if the pencil's not too heavy for him.

(LIZ *enters* R *with the sandals*)

LIZ. Will these do, Hugh?
HUGH (*moving* R) Perfect, darling.
LIZ. I hope they'll fit her.
HUGH (*taking the sandals and moving to the window*) May be just a shade big. Still, the thought's there. Thank you, darling. I'll call you if she's sunk in any further and wants jacking up.

(HUGH *exits* R)

LIZ (*moving* C) What's he been saying to you?
JOHN (*moving to the fire*) Telling me about your first kiss, that's all.
LIZ. Our first . . .
JOHN. In a Land Rover in Scotland—north of Carlisle—after fishing.
LIZ. John—he didn't . . .
JOHN. Yes, he did—and I don't find it very funny.
LIZ. Did he?
JOHN. I'm afraid so, riotously.
LIZ (*moving to the table* R) I'd had neat whisky with the fishing lunch as I was so wet.
JOHN. There's no need to make excuses.
LIZ. He's too naughty.
JOHN (*moving* C) He's too childish, if you ask me.
LIZ. I agree but never mind. He's got to keep up his morale somehow and that's the way he likes to do it.
JOHN. He'll be telling me about your honeymoon, I shouldn't wonder, next.
LIZ. I shouldn't either. (*Seeing that John has the photographs*) Did he talk about the children?
JOHN. Yes. He said that Sheila's going to be a push-over like you.
LIZ (*taking the photographs and moving down* L) And Dick?
JOHN. Dick's full of charm like him—but just about as lively as a tortoise.

(LIZ's *mouth twitches*)

It's not funny, Liz.
LIZ. No, John, you said that. (*She replaces the photographs up* L)
JOHN (*moving up* C) Let's go back to London. Come on, I can't stand this. Come on—let's get out of it. We'll have lunch on the way in some pub.
LIZ. No, John.
JOHN. Why not?

Liz. We can't run away.

John. I can't see why not. We're going to in the morning, anyway. So let's just put it forward twenty-four hours.

Liz. No, John.

John. But why not?

Liz (*moving down* L) It'd be the end, that's why not. If we can't take this, it means we can't take anything. We'd both be starting off with a defeat and that's not what I want to build our marriage on. We've got to go through with it.

John (*moving down* C) I suppose you're right.

Liz. Of course I'm right.

John (*moving* L *to Liz*) O.K., that's settled. But get this into your head. (*He takes her by the wrist*) If things get on your nerves, don't blame me.

Liz. That hurts, John.

John. It's meant to—to impress on you that staying here's your choice, and not mine.

Liz. Let me go please.

(John *lets her go.* Liz *moves to the sofa table and picks up a plate of nuts*)

John (*moving* C *below the sofa*) I can't tell you how I missed you last night.

Liz. Have a carrot?

John. What?

Liz. I meant a nut. I'm sorry, darling. I'm not concentrating. Everything's so confusing.

John. No it's not. It's clear as crystal. Come here.

(Liz *moves to John and they are about to embrace again*)

Hugh (*off*) Mind the step.

(Liz *moves down* R, John *to the fire.* Molly *enters* R)

Molly. Thanks so much for the sandals.

Liz. Not at all.

Molly. I think the garden's lovely.

(Hugh *enters with Molly's shoes*)

Hugh. Molly likes the blue delphiniums best. You should have a look at them, John.

John. I'd like to.

Liz. Not now Hugh—if you don't mind. It's almost lunchtime. (*To Molly*) Would you like to see your room?

Molly. Yes—thank you. (*She moves up* LC)

Liz. Hugh—will you show John his?

Hugh (*moving to the drinks table*) When I've topped myself up. Molly, my dear, don't forget your running shoes.

Molly. Oh, no. (*She turns back*) Thanks so much.

(MOLLY *exits*)

HUGH. Not at all, dear—I liked carrying them.

(LIZ *moves to the door*)

(*To Liz*) She came out quite easily. A good strong pull and then a squelch and there she was.

(LIZ *exits*)

(*To John*) I know just how a thrush feels now when it gets hold of a nice juicy worm. One for the stairs?
JOHN. No, thanks. (*He moves to the door*)
HUGH. Come on.
JOHN. Oh, all right, Walford. (*He moves L of Hugh*)
HUGH. Hugh's the name still.
JOHN. Hugh then—I'm your guest, I know, but I feel bound to tell you, you're behaving like a lunatic.
HUGH (*philosophically*) Maybe, but it's a mad world, isn't it? And I can never quite decide which side of the asylum wall's the inside.
JOHN (*ignoring this and moving to the table down* R) Liz and I are going off together and, although I'm sorry—looking at it from your point of view—there's nothing you can do about it.
HUGH (*on the old tack*) Do you know the one about the pigeon? (*He goes to John and gives him his drink*)
JOHN. Pigeon?
HUGH (*moving to the sofa and sitting*) That's right. And the lunatic. You brought the subject up not me. It illustrates my point about the difficulty of deciding who's sane and who isn't. Well, this lunatic was walking in the garden with a nurse, when this pigeon flew over. And it got him in the eye with a direct hit. In the lunatic's eye, got the picture?
JOHN. Yes. (*He moves* C)
HUGH. Good. And the nurse said "Hang on, I'll nip inside and get a bit of toilet paper!" Are you with me?
JOHN. Yes. (*He crosses below the sofa to the fire*)
HUGH. Well, here's the punch line. And the lunatic said, "Are you crazy, nurse, by the time you get back that bird'll be a mile away". Makes one think, old fellow, doesn't it? What was it you were saying? Ah yes—about you two packing off. Don't worry about that. I've got the message. That's why I'm behaving like I am. I'm trying to keep everybody happy. That's why I asked Molly down. To make a foursome, so that no one'd feel left out. I'd better show you your room now, or we'll be in trouble. (*He rises, takes John's glass and goes to the drinks table*) You're in my dressing-room—I hope you don't mind. Well, of course, you don't—why should you? It'll save a lot of mileage one way and another. And a lot of passage-navigation in a strange house in the dark's no fun at all. I knew a fellow once who used to go downstairs to dinner in a strange house with his valet

following behind and sticking drawing-pins in every board that creaked. He's dead now—and I'm not surprised. The chap—I mean. I wouldn't know about the valet. Probably still with us, as he must have got a lot of exercise.

(HUGH *moves to the door.* JOHN *follows*)

Right—off we go to Camp One.

(HUGH *opens the door,* LIZ *enters*)

Hullo, darling. Molly settled in all right?
LIZ. She seems quite happy.
HUGH. So she should be. After you, sir.
JOHN. Thank you.

(JOHN *goes out*)

HUGH. Did you put the champagne on the ice, dear?
LIZ. Mrs Gray did.
HUGH. Well done her—two bottles, I hope. I'm in festive mood.

(HUGH *exits.* LIZ *collects dirty sherry glasses from the table* R, *then moves down* L. MRS GRAY *enters with two bouquets, one of lilies and one of roses*)

MRS GRAY. These just came, Ma'am.
LIZ (*moving* C) Who for?
MRS GRAY. One's for you, the lilies.
LIZ. For me!

(MRS GRAY *shows Liz the bouquet of lilies*)

MRS GRAY. That's right, dear—from Mr Walford.

(LIZ *looks at the label*)

LIZ. And the roses?
MRS GRAY. For Miss Forsyth.
LIZ (*hastily, having seen her label*) Put them in some water in the flower-room, Mrs Gray. (*She goes to the drinks table*)
MRS GRAY (*moving* R) They're a picture, dear—and no mistake—I've seen them on the coffin at a funeral once, but I've never handled them before. 'Course these are lovely, too—I've got to say so. But it doesn't mean that I'm not shocked.
LIZ. Please, Mrs Gray, it's almost lunchtime.

(MRS GRAY *turns for the door.* HUGH *enters*)

HUGH. Ah, so they've arrived. Where are you going to put them, darling?
MRS GRAY (*indicating Miss Forsyth's bouquet of roses*) I know where I'd like to put this lot, sir—and that's in the dustbin.
HUGH. Mrs Gray, you're jealous.
MRS GRAY. Me—jealous—at my age—I like that.

HUGH (*persisting in pulling her leg*) You like that! (*Indicating the lilies*) And you'd like a bunch of these. Now, wouldn't you? Confess! Right, you shall have one, Mrs Gray.

MRS GRAY. It's no use trying to get round me.

HUGH. We'll see!

MRS GRAY. I'm plain disgusted with you if you want to know—and that's a fact.

(MRS GRAY *exits*. HUGH *goes over to the telephone*)

LIZ. How could you, Hugh? (*She moves down* C)

HUGH. Quite easily—Interflora. I rang up Constance Spry before I started for the Golf Club. (*He dials*)

LIZ. Who're you ringing now? (*She sits on the sofa*)

HUGH. A girl friend.

LIZ. Aren't you satisfied with one?

HUGH. No. I've become insatiable. (*He is holding on*) She's smashing, Molly—isn't she? And most accommodating. So they tell me. Rumour has it she went through my publisher's office like a circular —and still good friends with everyone—That's what I'm looking for—I'm through with love—it lets you down—it's unreliable. From now on, it's champagne and dalliance for me—and laughter. Life's too short to dig down any deeper. (*He takes the telephone to the sofa and sits on the* R *arm*) Hullo, Constance Spry? . . . Ah, good—Hugh Walford speaking—I rang earlier this morning . . . Yes—indeed they have—and they're lovely. Thank you very much. I'd like to have the same again in lilies, if you don't mind . . . That's right. Mrs Gray—A—Y. The same address, yes . . . What? The card? Oh, yes—what did we have the first time? . . . "All my love, Hugh". Yes, that's all right if you put a "Walford" on the end. I don't know her so well as I know Mrs Walford. And slip in a dozen roses as well. To John Brownlow . . . Yes, I did say John . . . Yes, same address and same card. Without "Walford" on the end. Just "all my love, Hugh" . . . Thank you so much. Have a nice week-end. Where are you going to? . . . Yes—I see. Well, be careful of the jelly-fish. Good-bye, dear. (*He hangs up*) What a nice girl—I can think of much worse things than being bedded out by her. (*He returns the telephone to the desk*) Well, everybody's fixed up now—except for Mr Gray and he can pick his own. So let's hope there'll be no more jealousy.

LIZ. How many gin-and-tonics have you had?

HUGH. I've lost count, but thank you for reminding me (*He goes to the drinks table*)

LIZ. You're being very silly, Hugh.

HUGH. We all are, aren't we? What about a touch more sherry?

LIZ. No thanks.

HUGH. Come on, you're behaving like a disapproving governess.

LIZ. And you're behaving like a spoilt child.

HUGH (*refusing to be ruffled*) Come on.

Liz. No, I said.

Hugh. What were you planning for this afternoon?

Liz. Don't ask me—you invited them.

Hugh. I thought a little snooze myself to set the caviare. (*He moves* RC) And then I thought I might take Molly swimming in the Jessel's pool.

Liz. You've asked them, have you?

Hugh. They're in the South of France. But David said we could go any time. Provided that we put the lilos in the changing-room and locked the door.

Liz. I'm sure you'll do that.

Hugh. What do you and John plan doing?

Liz. I don't know—I haven't asked him.

Hugh. You could watch the racing on the television or play croquet.

Liz. Thank you.

Hugh. Or perhaps he's got his own ideas. A nice chap, isn't he? Damned near the perfect athlete, I should say. It's not surprising he's collected all those wives.

Liz. Hugh.

Hugh. Yes, my darling.

Liz. If you think that your extraordinary behaviour's going to have the least effect on me, you'd better think again.

Hugh. I will if necessary.

(MOLLY *enters in trousers, looking a dish*)

Ah, Molly—well, well—that's a sight for sore eyes. Can I tempt you? (*He indicates the drinks*)

Molly. No, thanks—I've had quite enough.

Hugh (*moving* L) I've just been telling Liz—I thought I'd take you swimming in the afternoon when I've had my siesta.

Molly. Oh, how lovely. Is it near here?

Hugh. Five miles—through the lanes.

Molly (*moving* R) What fun. I hope you're coming, Mrs Walford.

Hugh. No, she isn't. John and Liz are going to play a little gentle croquet.

(JOHN *enters and moves* R *of the drinks table*)

Molly. I love croquet.

Hugh. So they tell me. Here you are, John. Just time for a quick one.

John. No, thanks.

Hugh. Come on. You'll be swilling down that damned Chianti next week, longing for a decent drop of gin-and-tonic. (*He goes to the drinks table*) Molly's going off to Italy tomorrow too.

John. Oh really—what part?

Molly. Venice—Florence—Rome . . .

Hugh. She likes a bit of sculpture, don't you, Molly?

Molly. Well—yes. (*She moves down* r)

Hugh. And a bit of architecture—and a bit of painting—and a bit of everything, in fact. I've just been telling Liz, we're going swimming in the afternoon at a friend's pool.

John. Oh, that sounds just the ticket. It's the perfect day for it.

Hugh. Well, it's the perfect day for everything. That's why I'm leaving you and Liz here with the croquet lawn at your disposal.

John. Oh, fine.

Liz. If you'd rather go and swim, John—we'll all go together.

Hugh. No, no. You stay here. You're going to get a lot of swimming when you're in Italy. But poor old Molly hoofing round the Doge's Palace and me in my study—we're the ones who want to take advantage of the sun. (*He moves to the sofa table*) I just can't wait to go in at the deep end—can you, Molly—you in your bikini and me in my water-wings!

(Mrs Gray *enters with the lilies in a vase*)

Mrs Gray (*moving* l *of Liz*) I've brought them in, dear. They're so lovely that I couldn't bear to waste them for another minute.

Liz (*indicating the sofa table*) Put them down there Mrs Gray—and I'll find the best place for them. Thank you. Is lunch ready?

Mrs Gray (*at the sofa table*) Nearly, Ma'am.

Hugh. Have you arranged Miss Forsyth's roses?

Mrs Gray. No, sir.

Hugh. Why not?

Mrs Gray. I've not had the time, sir. (*She moves to the door*)

Hugh (*thundering*) Find time, Mrs Gray.

Mrs Gray. Yes, sir.

(Mrs Gray *exits quaking*)

Hugh. Women like a bit of domination. Keep the voice as low as possible and kick them in the teeth and you're in clover. (*He moves down* r *to Molly*) I'm so sorry, but she's jealous.

Molly. I don't understand.

(John *moves to the fire*)

Hugh. What don't you understand, my dear?

Molly. Who's sent me roses.

Hugh. I have.

Molly. You have!

Hugh. Yes—two dozen.

Molly. But whatever for?

(Mrs Gray *enters with roses in one hand and a vase in the other*)

Hugh. Because I find you very charming—that accounts for the first dozen. And I find you most attractive. That covers the second. May I? (*He kisses her on the cheek*) Thank you.

MOLLY (*moving* R *of Mrs Gray*) Oh, how lovely. Are they really for me? (*She takes the roses*)
HUGH. Every one of them, my dear. (*He takes the roses*)
MOLLY. Oh, thank you.

(MOLLY *embraces and kisses Hugh*)

HUGH. Fifteen all, my service—

(HUGH *kisses Molly.* MOLLY *moves upstage a pace.* HUGH *takes the vase from Mrs Gray*)

Thank you, Mrs Gray.
MRS GRAY. That's quite all right, sir.
HUGH (*moving to the table down* R *and arranging the roses*) You can have a teaspoonful of caviare as a reward and half a glass of champagne.
MRS GRAY. Thank you, sir.
HUGH. Don't mention it.
MRS GRAY. And lunch is in, Ma'am.
LIZ (*rising and moving above the sofa*) Thank you, Mrs Gray.

(MRS GRAY *goes*)

MOLLY. And who gave you those, Mrs Walford?
LIZ (*lying*) Mr Brownlow.
MOLLY. They're lovely, too—but I like roses best.
HUGH (*letting Liz get away with it*) I thought you would, dear. I find lilies just a shade funereal. (*He improves the arrangement of the roses*) They're beautiful of course—but faintly sad—like a memorial. A kind of "thank you" for the past. Whereas I always think of roses as a promise for the future; don't you, John? (*He moves to the sofa table*)
JOHN. I've never thought about it.
HUGH (*moving upstage*) Oh well, you will, you will.
LIZ (*coldly*) We'll find a place for those two vases after lunch, Hugh. (*She moves to the door and waits*) Come along, Miss Forsyth.

(MOLLY *waits for Liz to go first*)

No, no, after you, dear.
MOLLY. Thank you.

(MOLLY *exits, followed by* LIZ. JOHN *moves to the door, but hesitates, as Molly did.* HUGH *beckons him forward*)

HUGH. No, no—after you, Johnski!

JOHN *starts to exit, as—*

the CURTAIN *falls*

ACT II

SCENE I

SCENE—*The same. Late on Saturday night.*
Moonlight can be seen in the garden through any openings in the window curtains. Another fine vase of red roses stands on table R, *waiting to be pinpointed.*

When the CURTAIN *rises,* JOHN, LIZ, HUGH *and* MOLLY *are playing bridge on a table set below the sofa.* MOLLY *is sitting on the sofa,* LIZ *on the upstage chair,* HUGH *on a chair* L, *and* JOHN *on the downstage chair. The men wear dinner-jackets, and* JOHN *has his cummerbund. The women are in evening gowns. Hands are being arranged.*

HUGH. One no trump.
JOHN. Double.
MOLLY. Two Hearts.
LIZ. Three Clubs.
HUGH. Three Hearts.
JOHN. Four Clubs.
MOLLY. Four Hearts.
LIZ. Double.
HUGH. Content.
JOHN. No.
HUGH (*to Liz*) Your lead, Liz—four Hearts.
MOLLY (*to John*) Oh, dear—I hope you've got something.
HUGH. You'd be surprised, my dear.

(LIZ *leads.* HUGH *puts down his hand*)

Four Hearts, and if you get it, that's the rubber. (*He rises*) Anybody thirsty?
LIZ. I'd like a bitter lemon if there is one.
HUGH. Molly?
MOLLY. No thanks, I'm far too excited.
HUGH (*moving to the drinks table*) Good girl. Take it steady, my dear—and count trumps. There tend to be around thirteen in most packs. You, John?
JOHN. No, thanks.
HUGH (*pouring Liz's drink*) Who took that trick?
MOLLY. I did.
HUGH. Well done—keep it up. There's lots more where that came from.
LIZ. Be quiet, Hugh—you're cheating.
HUGH (*giving Liz her drink*) Sorry, darling.

LIZ. Thank you.

HUGH. There's a lot of people walking the Embankment, so they say, who never took trumps out.

(LIZ, MOLLY and JOHN *continue to play*)

LIZ. Hugh, if you don't stop talking, I'll throw my hand in.

(MRS GRAY *comes in carrying her bouquet of lilies*)

HUGH (*moving* RC) Come in, Mrs Gray. Don't worry Mrs Walford at the moment—we're playing four hearts doubled. Have a drink while you're waiting?

MRS GRAY. No, sir—thank you all the same.

HUGH (*moving to the drinks table*) Well, you won't mind if I do.

MRS GRAY. Thank you for the lovely flowers, sir.

HUGH. Not at all. (*He pours himself a drink*) I'm glad you liked them.

MRS GRAY. They're lovely. But you never should have done it. Mr Gray says they're the most expensive flowers that you can buy—especially in London.

HUGH. He's got something there. (*There is a pause while the bridge continues*) Well, let's do my department while we're waiting, shall we? I'll have my usual cup of tea at seven-thirty.

MRS GRAY. Yes, sir.

HUGH. And I'm sure that that'll suit Miss Forsyth as she's got to be in London early. Molly, my dear—are you very busy?

MOLLY. I'm just thinking.

HUGH. Sorry.

MOLLY. Why, what is it? You've distracted me now!

HUGH. What train are you catching in the morning?

MOLLY. Ten-five.

HUGH. Yes, I thought so. That's the only one there is. And Indian or China?

MOLLY. China, please.

HUGH. Good. That'll save a lot of trouble, won't it, Mrs Gray? One teapot and two cups at seven-thirty in the spare room. And a Rich Tea biscuit, or two.

MOLLY (*referring to a finesse that has succeeded*) Got it! And the rest are mine. (*She throws her cards face up on the table*)

HUGH (*moving* L *of Molly*) Well done, dear.

MOLLY. Well, all the finesses came off.

HUGH. Most unusual.

MOLLY. What's that make it?

HUGH. Four Hearts doubled—two hundred and forty. And five hundred for the rubber. And another fifty for the insult.

MOLLY. Oh, how lovely.

(*There is a pause*)

HUGH (*to Liz*) Darling—(*indicating Mrs Gray's presence*)—Mrs Gray.

I've done the early morning order for my section—what about you?
(*He moves to the french windows*)

Liz. Just knock on my door at half-past seven, Mrs Gray—as usual.

Mrs Gray. Yes, Ma'am.

Liz. John—do you like early morning tea?

John (*rising*) No, thank you—never touch it. (*He takes Hugh's chair* L *of the door*)

Liz. Well, then—breakfast—nine on, down here. How would that suit everybody?

Molly. Perfect, yes.

John. Fine. (*He moves above the sofa table*)

Hugh (*moving* c) Dressing-gowns for those who haven't been to Early Service.

Liz. Thank you, Mrs Gray. Good night.

Mrs Gray. Good night, Ma'am. Good night, Sir. Good night, Miss.

Molly. Good night, Mrs Gray.

Mrs Gray (*mellowed towards Hugh since the flowers*) Good night, sir.

Hugh. Good night, Mrs Gray.

(Mrs Gray *exits*)

Well, that's the way to treat an Amazon—say it with flowers. Now, what's the damage, John?

John (*getting out his money*) I make it twenty.

Liz. Oh—I've left my money upstairs in my other bag.

Hugh. Don't worry, darling, I'll fix it.

(John *gives Hugh a ten-shilling note*)

Thank you, John. (*He passes it on to Molly*) That's Liz's debt to you, my dear.

Molly. But what about you?

Hugh. Never mind me—it's the last time I'll be paying up for her —apart from alimony. Please forgive me, Molly, if I talk shop for a moment, as there won't be much time in the morning. I'll be giving Liz a divorce, John—I don't know if she told you? (*He moves* rc)

John. Well, yes, she did mention it this afternoon.

Hugh. Oh, good. And I'll be as generous as possible, of course— allowing for the children and the Chancellor. And you're pretty well endowed, from what I gather—and she's not expensive.

Liz. Darling, anyone'd think I was your daughter from the way you're talking!

Hugh. Quite a lot of people have thought that, my darling—in the past. That's been the trouble. Any of your past wives been much younger than you, John?

John (*moving down* l) The second one was.

Hugh. How old?

JOHN. Seventeen. (*He sits down* L)

HUGH. Oh dear—that's stretching it a bit. What was she: Mexican?

JOHN. No, Austrian.

HUGH. How long did she last?

JOHN. Two years.

HUGH. What went wrong?

LIZ. Hugh, really! Anyone'd think you were a psychoanalyst.

HUGH (*moving John's card-table chair* R *of the french windows then returning* C) I sometimes think I should have been one—writing makes one very analytical, you know—one couldn't be one if one weren't. One sees everything from outside quite impersonally—one's own life just the same as other people's. For instance, I can see four people in this room quite clearly—not three. Maybe that's what makes me difficult to live with. Look at Liz, poor darling, she's been living with a typewriter to all intents and purposes for fifteen years. (*He moves* R) And typewriters aren't good in bed—apart from all their other failings—twisted tape and three-quarters instead of question marks! (*He has arrived beside John's flowers*) I hope you like them, John—you never thanked me for them. When did they arrive?

JOHN. This afternoon.

LIZ. When you were swimming at the Jessel's pool.

HUGH (*picking up the roses and moving* C) Ah, yes, I see—and you forgot about them—fair enough. Or, were you annoyed?

JOHN. No, of course not.

HUGH. Sure?

JOHN. Of course I'm sure.

HUGH. You didn't mind the note?

JOHN. No. (*He rises and moves up* L)

HUGH. "All my love, Hugh"! (*He replaces the flowers* R) Took that in his stride, Liz, did he?

LIZ. Yes, of course, Hugh.

HUGH. I'll bet he didn't. (*Moving to the desk*) I'll bet he snorted and then tore it up and threw it in the basket. Any takers? (*He picks up a crumpled card from the waste-paper basket*) Hullo, hullo—what's this, John, old fellow? (*Reading*) "All my love, Hugh". Crumpled, thrown away, rejected, spurned—I hoped you'd stick it in your wallet underneath the dollar-clip, and look at it each night before you went to bed, and thank God that there's no ill-feeling.

JOHN (*moving to Hugh*) I'm afraid I didn't take it very seriously.

HUGH. Why not? That was a mistake.

JOHN. I just thought you were being funny.

HUGH. Dear, oh dear! What made you think that—just because I write light novels. Dear, oh dear—you mustn't be so superficial, John, you really mustn't. Even my son Dick knows clowns tread water in their own tears all their lives, and he's a schoolboy. I was being serious, old chap. Those roses represent my olive branch, my pipe of peace—and, since they won't survive for long, this little card's my draft peace treaty.

(*Hugh holds out the card and* JOHN *takes it*)

JOHN. Thank you. (*He takes the card, puts it in his wallet, and moves down* R *to sit in the armchair*)

HUGH (*watching John*) Thank you. I apologize for giving the impression I was being funny. That's the penalty for being different in a uniform world—I can't help it. It's the way I'm made.

LIZ (*rising*) I think I'll go up, if you don't mind. What about you, Molly?

MOLLY. Well, I . . .

HUGH (*moving down* C) No, no—Molly doesn't want to go yet, do you, Molly? We're going to go and listen for a nightingale out in the orchard—planned it all this afternoon, when we were swimming, didn't we—she's never heard one. (*He picks up a light cardigan, off the downstage arm of the sofa*) Come along, my dear, is this yours? You may need it.

MOLLY (*getting up*) Yes. (*She moves to Hugh*)

HUGH (*helping her on with it*) Good. (*To Liz*) Don't go up yet, darling—stay and talk to John. It is your last night, after all, at home. We won't be long, and we must have a night-cap; just to show there's no ill-feeling. (*To Molly*) Ready, dear?

MOLLY. Yes, Hugh.

HUGH. Good. Lead on. Mind the step.

(MOLLY *exits through the french windows*)

(*Moving to John and whispering*) Amazing—she spends half her life in Berkeley Square and yet she's never heard a nightingale.

(HUGH *follows Molly out*)

LIZ. He's going to do it, John. (*She places her card-table chair* R *of the door*)

JOHN. Do what? (*He rises and moves to the windows*)

LIZ. Provide me with the evidence. (*Moving to the card-table*) He ordered tea for two from Mrs Gray at seven-thirty.

JOHN. Yes—I heard him. (*Moving* R *of the card-table*) That's what made me lead the wrong card.

(JOHN *and* LIZ *clear the cards*)

LIZ. It's disgusting—in his own house!

JOHN. Still, if that's the way he wants it done—why should we worry? (*He takes the cards and glass to the desk*)

LIZ. He's my husband, John.

JOHN. Yes, darling.

LIZ (*starting to fold up the card-table*) After fifteen years! He's never looked to right or left before. And now he's ready to jump into bed with that appalling girl.

JOHN (*returning to the card-table*) I don't think she's all that appalling. (*He takes the table and continues folding it*)

LIZ. No, of course you don't—you're a man—and men have got no taste. You're animals, that's all you are. If you think something's pretty, that's enough for you—you're utterly, completely superficial —all of you!

JOHN. Thanks very much. (*He turns upstage with the table*)

LIZ (*taking the table from John, putting it behind the drinks table, then returning down* L) Whereas a woman can see through a girl like that at once. She's money-grubbing, over-sexed—in fact, she's almost certainly a nymphomaniac.

JOHN. Well—I'm not arguing. (*He sits on the sofa*)

LIZ. How can he even contemplate it, John?

JOHN. Don't ask me.

LIZ. If he wants to give me a divorce—and there's no reason why he should when he can easily divorce me—but still, if he wants to, out of a mistaken sense of chivalry—(*moving down* R)—why can't he go to Brighton like a normal person, with a normal woman—instead of indulging in this beastly exhibition in his own home with that dreadful little creature.

JOHN. I don't think she's all that dreadful.

LIZ. Don't keep saying that!

JOHN. I'm sorry, darling—but I see old Hugh's point.

LIZ. Trust you! (*She sits on the stool*)

JOHN. And in fairness I must say so—I mean, why go off to Brighton with a lady in a leopard-skin coat in her fifties, when you've got a girl who's obviously keen on you, who won't be doing *The Times* crossword all night in an arm-chair, by the gasfire. (*Rising and moving up* C) Why go off to the Municipal Baths when you've got a private swimming pool?

LIZ. You're talking just like Hugh.

JOHN (*moving down* C) I'm sorry. I'm afraid the most attractive man in London's letting you down. What on earth made you say that about me?

LIZ. I got furious with Hugh pretending he'd never heard of you.

JOHN (*sitting on the* R *arm of the sofa*) So you indulged yourself in wishful thinking.

LIZ (*rising and moving up* R; *ignoring this argument*) Do you realize Hugh's over fifty, John?

JOHN. That's right.

LIZ (*moving down* C) What do you mean—"that's right"?

JOHN. I was confirming your assessment of his age, that's all.

LIZ. And Molly's twenty-five, at the outside.

JOHN. That could be right, too.

LIZ. Can't you see it's quite out of the question?

JOHN. On the drawing-board, perhaps—but not in practice. Maybe he's just what she's looking for—some women like them old—and vice-versa.

LIZ. You must stop him, John.

JOHN. I hardly think I'm quite in a position to.

LIZ. If you don't, I will.

JOHN. I see—how do you propose to do that?

LIZ. By appealing to his better nature.

JOHN (*rising and moving to the fire*) Well, good luck to you.

LIZ. If you stay down here, talking to him, after we've gone up—and you must—otherwise he'll get into that spare room dressing-room, and he might lock the door—then I'll come down again, and you must go to bed, and leave us.

JOHN. I'll be glad to, darling.

LIZ (*moving to John*) Yes, of course you will—you're all alike, you men—you stick together like glue. If you had an ounce of guts, you'd talk to him yourself and make him so ashamed he'd curl up on the sofa for the night instead of going upstairs to that . . . (*she pauses to find an adequate word for Molly's inadequacy, and moves up L*)

JOHN (*cutting in*) You're jealous, Liz.

LIZ. Me—jealous?

JOHN. Yes.

LIZ. Don't be silly. (*She moves up RC*)

JOHN. Well, possessive, if you like—but it's the same thing. You can't bear what's been your property for years on someone else's mantelpiece. (*Moving L of Liz*) You've got to face it, though—you've got to learn that Hugh's entitled to conduct his life exactly as he pleases once you've left him. If he wants to keep a harem here, you haven't any right to stop him. If you can't accept that, we'd better call the whole thing off—because it's not on.

LIZ. No, John—you don't mean that, do you?

JOHN. I'm afraid I do.

LIZ. No, darling—say you don't. Please say you don't. You've got to say you don't.

JOHN. All right—but pull yourself together—otherwise you'll lose the pair of us.

LIZ. You didn't mean that, darling?

JOHN. We'll see.

LIZ. What do you mean by that?

JOHN (*moving C*) Exactly what I say—you're either Hugh's or mine—you can't be both. You've got to make the break—the final break.

LIZ. I've made it, John.

JOHN. All right—but don't keep looking back—or it'll make you dizzy.

LIZ. I can talk to him, though—can't I?

JOHN. I suppose so—if you must.

LIZ (*moving down RC*) I must, John.

JOHN (*moving down C*) All right—but remember what I've said. It's Hugh—or me. And, if it's me—it isn't Hugh in any way—not even as a self-appointed supervisor of his sex-life. (*Trying to lighten the atmosphere*) How would that be as a bit of dialogue in one of his books?

LIZ (*sulkily, hearing footsteps outside*) You'd better ask him.

(John *moves down* l, *and* Liz *down* r. Molly *enters from the french windows*)

Molly. We heard one. (*She moves to the stool*)
Liz (*forcing civility*) Oh, well done.
Molly (*sitting on the stool*) It was too lovely.

(Hugh *enters*)

Hugh (*moving* c) Singing fit to bust itself—you ought to hear it, John.
John. I'd like to.
Hugh. Take him down there, darling—just beyond the summer-house—the far end of that clump of saplings.
John (*moving* lc) Don't you bother—I'll go.
Hugh. No—I don't want you ploughing through the border like a wounded buffalo. You take him, darling—it's worth hearing.
Molly (*offering her woolly*) Would you like this?

(Hugh *moves to the drinks table*)

Liz. Thank you. (*To Hugh*) Where are you going, Hugh?
Hugh. To get the drinks. What would you like, my darling?
Liz. Nothing, thank you.
Hugh. Come on—we must have a farewell drink together. That's one reason why I've got this bottle on the ice. (*He picks up a champagne bottle*)
Liz. Oh, all right—just a drop, though.

(Liz *exits through the french windows*)

Hugh. You, John?
John. Half a glass'll do me.

(John *moves to the window, trips on the step, and exits*)

Hugh. Right, sir. Mind the step. (*Shouting to John*) And sing a bit yourself if it won't play. They can't stand rivalry. What would you like, my dear?
Molly (*rising and moving to the sofa*) A drop of champagne, please. (*She sits* l *on the sofa*)
Hugh (*starting to open the bottle*) I've given you a dreadful reputation with those two—I hope you don't mind.
Molly. Oh dear—what have you said?
Hugh. Well, I've left Liz with the idea that you're most accommodating.
Molly. And did she believe it?
Hugh. I sincerely hope so.
Molly. It won't work.
Hugh. I wonder. (*The cork pops*) Anyway, it's very nice of you to play.
Molly. I don't appear to have had much alternative.

HUGH (*pouring*) I told her you'd been right through my publisher's office like a circular.

MOLLY. Thanks very much.

HUGH. And that you were still friends with all of them.

MOLLY. Well, that's nice, anyway.

HUGH. And that you had a passion for me.

MOLLY. Oh, how did you guess?

HUGH. And that I'm going to give her evidence for the divorce by being found in bed with you by Mrs Gray tomorrow morning, when she brings the China tea and Rich Tea biscuits in at seven-thirty.

MOLLY. I love Rich Tea biscuits . . .

HUGH. Oh, well, that'll be a point of contact. And I'm sleeping in the spare room dressing-room communicating with your room. (*He picks up two glasses*)

MOLLY. I guessed that when I heard you singing before dinner.

HUGH. And you mustn't lock the intervening door.

MOLLY. Why not?

HUGH (*moving to the sofa and sitting R of Molly*) Because I'm too big to get through the keyhole.

MOLLY. So you're going to pay a social call? (*She takes her glass*)

HUGH. Yes.

MOLLY. What time?

HUGH. Any time that suits you.

MOLLY. Seven twenty-seven.

HUGH. Not before that!

MOLLY. No, Hugh.

HUGH. Why not?

MOLLY. I'll be asleep.

HUGH. I thought of that. So I planned coming in before you went to sleep tonight.

MOLLY. Oh, did you?

HUGH. Yes—with champagne and what Mrs Gray's left of the caviare.

MOLLY. What purpose would that serve?

HUGH. A very good one. Liz is sure to come along and peep into the dressing room at some time in the night or other—and it wouldn't do for her to find me there, snoring my head off, would it?

MOLLY. Why not?

HUGH. You know damned well why not.

MOLLY. But it would do if she heard you snoring your head off in my room—through the intervening door?

HUGH. Precisely—are you playing?

MOLLY (*rising and moving down L*) What do I get out of it?

HUGH. Champagne and caviare.

MOLLY. And nothing else?

HUGH. No—not unless you want it. If you want a grape, or something, naturally I'll nip down for it.

MOLLY. Thank you. (*She crosses down R*)

HUGH. Is it on then?

MOLLY. How loud do you snore?

HUGH. Depends on whether I'm asleep, or not.

MOLLY (*moving to the armchair* R) When you're asleep.

HUGH. Not too bad. You'll merely think you're crossing prematurely to Boulogne tomorrow in a heat haze.

MOLLY. That sounds rather restful.

HUGH. Yes, it could be—Well?

MOLLY. All right, Hugh.

HUGH. You're a good girl.

MOLLY (*sitting in the armchair*) Don't forget that.

(LIZ *enters* R)

HUGH (*rising and moving up* C) Hullo—did you hear it?

LIZ. Yes.

(JOHN *enters and moves up* R)

HUGH. A good sound, isn't it, John? (*He hands John a glass*)

JOHN. Fabulous, yes. (*He takes the glass*)

HUGH. Funny way of getting through the night. Still, if we all did that, I reckon it'd save a bit of trouble. Think of Johnski, sitting on the bed-post in his mews flat, with his cummerbund contracting and expanding and his Adam's apple going sixteen to the dozen. (*He raises his glass*) Well, good luck in Italy—and in the future.

(LIZ *takes the glass from Hugh, moves to the sofa and sits*)

JOHN. Thank you—and the same to you.

HUGH. Don't worry about me. I'm going to have myself a ball. I'm feeling like a convict coming out of Dartmoor after fifteen years. (*To John*) I see why you've cut down your marriages to size, old chap. It's definitely not an institution that wants over-emphasizing—not unless you want to finish up a vegetable. (*He moves to the fire. To Liz*) That's what I've been for years, Liz. I was thinking in my bath tonight—a bloody vegetable. Well, that's no damned good for a novelist. He ought to be outside the kitchen garden, in among the roses and the lilies of the valley.

LIZ (*rising*) Are you coming, Molly? (*She moves up* C, *putting her glass on the sofa table*)

MOLLY (*rising*) Yes—I think I will. (*To John*) Good night. (*She moves to the door*)

JOHN. Good night, Miss Forsyth.

MOLLY. Good night, Hugh.

(MOLLY *exits*)

HUGH. Good night, my darling.

LIZ. Good night, John.

(LIZ *exits*)

JOHN. Good night, Liz.
HUGH. Good night, Liz, sleep well.

(JOHN *moves to the drinks table*)

HUGH. One for the stairs?
JOHN. No, thank you.
HUGH (*moving to the drinks table*) Come on! Give them time to take
their faces off, good Heavens! (*He pours some more into John's glass*)
Nothing's killed romance so much, in the last fifty years, in my
opinion, as men going up to bed at the same time as women. Well, it
stands to reason. Who wants some great purple-faced baboon lying
in bed behind them when they're working on the Ponds Cold Cream!

(JOHN *sits on the sofa.* HUGH *moves to the fire*)

And what man's going to be a demon lover after hearing bottles
clicking on a glass-topped dressing table like machine-gun fire for
half the night? I wouldn't be surprised if it's not that that's got the
sexes all botched up. You mark my words, young fellow, if it goes on,
by the year two-thousand—I'd reckon you'd need a radar set to tell
the sexes apart. Our grandfathers weren't fools, you know. They
came upstairs, topped up with brandy and they found their women
waiting for them—whether they were theirs or someone else's they
were waiting for them. Do I make myself clear? (*He moves to John*)
JOHN. Amply.

(JOHN *rises, but* HUGH *puts his hand on John's shoulder and they sit
side by side on the sofa*)

HUGH. I'll tell you something, Johnski. Sometimes Liz'll sit on
that damned dressing-table stool till after midnight—firing intermit-
tent bursts with those damned bottles on the glass top. And then, by
the time she's berthed alongside me—I'm sunk without trace. (*He
puts his hand on John's leg*) You watch that, my boy, in Italy—she
doesn't like it. Take my tip and stay downstairs in the hotel until they
turn the lights out in the lounge—don't take the lift—go up the stairs
by easy stages, smoking a last cigarette and, even then, you'll be too
early nine times out of ten. I'll tell you what to do then—get into the
bath—that's if she's out of it—if not, it's naturally a different story—
if she is, though, jump in and lie soaking in it—never mind the
indigestion—till she calls you. Then don't answer. She'll call again in
a few minutes, "Hugh—sorry, I mean John, what are you doing, darling?"—and don't answer again. Then she'll call a third time. This
time answer casually, though. Just say, "Coming, darling". Then
get out and dry and nip into the bedroom. It's the only way to stay on
top—perhaps I could have put that better. But you see what I mean?
(*He rises and moves R to the stool*)
JOHN. Yes, I take the point.
HUGH. It's over-rated, isn't it?
JOHN. What?

HUGH. Sex, in general.

JOHN. Well, that's a point of view.

HUGH. Which you don't share?

JOHN. No, not entirely—not at all, in fact.

HUGH (*sitting on the stool*) You're quite a dab at it, so they tell me?

JOHN. Who do?

HUGH. No one, old chap. Don't misunderstand me. It's just my assumption—based on what I know about you.

JOHN. On my marriages, you mean?

HUGH. Yes—three—would that be right?

JOHN. Quite right.

HUGH. Why did you marry them?

JOHN. Instead of living with them, do you mean?

HUGH. Yes, that's right.

JOHN. I'm a marrying man.

HUGH. Fair enough. Why leave them, then?

JOHN. Quite simple. I got bored with them.

HUGH. In what way?

JOHN. All ways.

HUGH. Mentally and physically?

JOHN. Yes, both.

HUGH. But which, predominantly?

JOHN. Well . . .

HUGH. I'll tell you—physically.

JOHN. Perhaps.

HUGH. You wanted a change.

JOHN. Possibly.

HUGH. Like someone who's been playing damned well on St George's for a long time and he thinks he ought to have a go at Prince's!

JOHN. If you like.

HUGH. You're a professional, in fact—an expert. You're so highly skilled that every now and then, you want to try your woods and your long irons on a different set of bunkers and a different set of greens.

JOHN. You put things very picturesquely.

HUGH (*rising and moving* RC) But why become a Member each time, old boy? Why not pay your green fees and then have whatever rounds you feel like?

JOHN. Members have a lot of prestige.

HUGH. For example?

JOHN. A good conscience.

HUGH. Bless my soul, you really meant that, didn't you?

JOHN. Of course I did.

HUGH (*moving above the sofa and down* L *of it*) Do you know, if I put you in a book—a fellow with three wives and a fourth on the drawing-board—and made you say the reason why you acted like an amateur Mohammedan was conscience, no one would believe me. They'd think it was a bad joke, but the truth is it's a very good joke—the best sort of joke of all, because it's true. (*He sits on the sofa*) I love you, Johnski, you're honest and straightforward and I love an honest and straightforward man. You're worth a bench of Bishops. Every time you love a woman, you get married. Do you know, you should be canonized.

JOHN. Are you being sarcastic?

HUGH. No. You've taught me so much in the last ten minutes. You've made "love your enemies" a sensible suggestion. But what about Liz?

JOHN. What about her?

HUGH. I don't want you getting bored with her.

JOHN. I won't—don't worry.

HUGH. You thought that before—with all the other ones.

JOHN. Yes, that's true. But I'm older now.

HUGH. And wiser?

JOHN. Much, much wiser.

HUGH. Well, you've had some cramming, certainly.

JOHN. Besides, it isn't only physical with her.

HUGH (*putting his arm round John*) I doubt if she'd agree. You see, old fellow, let's face it, I'm a pretty poor performer in that line. You don't mind me talking to you like this, do you?

JOHN. I'm beginning to get used to it.

HUGH. That's most broadminded of you. Well, what I was going to say was that—in that particular sphere, you make rings round me, I should imagine—like you do at golf. Don't think I'm criticizing you, for Heaven's sake—I'm merely stating facts. That being so— once you turned up behind that cocktail glass at that damned Embassy and hit it off with Liz—the game was up. There wasn't anything that I could do about it except smooth your passage so to speak. We're on two different wavelengths—yours is physical and mine is mental, broadly speaking. And the trouble from my point of view is that my batteries are running down. Well, they're bound to for a lot of reasons—age, for one, and lack of distilled water for another, and a little too much distilled whisky for a third! It therefore follows that my signals, on my wife's receiving set, are getting weaker, even if you weren't jamming me—and yours are coming over, loud and clear. And that's why I concede defeat with no hard feelings. (*He raises his glass*) Good luck. God speed. (*He kisses John on the top of the head*)

    (LIZ *enters*)

(*rising and moving to the fire*) Hullo, darling—what's the matter?

LIZ. I came down to get my travellers' cheques. (*She goes to the desk*)

HUGH. Oh, yes—you'll need them. And your passport. Don't forget your passport.

JOHN (*rising and moving to the drinks table*) Well, I think I'll go to bed.

HUGH. Poor Johnski never got a word in edgeways. That's what happens when the most attractive man in London meets the most long-winded man in Hampshire head-on!

JOHN. Good night, Liz.

LIZ. Good night, John.

HUGH. Don't forget your roses.

JOHN (*embarrassed*) I'll take them in the morning.

HUGH. No, no take them up. I'll be most hurt if you don't take them.

(JOHN *collects the flowers and moves to the door*)

John, what time are you due at Lympne?

JOHN. Twelve-thirty, isn't it, Liz?

LIZ. Yes, I think so.

HUGH. Oh, well, if you leave about a quarter to ten you'll do it easily.

(HUGH *moves to the door*)

LIZ. Where are you going, Hugh?

HUGH. To get the caviare—good night, John.

(HUGH *exits*)

JOHN (*calling after him*) Good night.

HUGH (*off*) Sleep well.

LIZ. What has he been saying?

JOHN. Quite a lot—I'll tell you upstairs, darling.

LIZ. John, I've locked my door.

JOHN. Whatever for?

LIZ. Because I'm tired.

JOHN. Oh, I see—all right—good night. (*He turns for the door, carrying the flowers*)

LIZ. Let me take those up—you look too silly carrying them.

JOHN (*as dignified as possible in the circumstances*) I'm all right, thanks.

LIZ. Aren't you going to kiss me?

JOHN. No.

(JOHN *exits*)

LIZ (*moving to the door*) Johnski . . .

(HUGH *enters, leaving the door open, and carrying the caviare and a spoon.* LIZ *moves to the table down* R. HUGH *moves to the sofa table*)

HUGH. Found them, darling?

LIZ. Yes—I've got them.

HUGH. And the passport?

LIZ. Yes.

(HUGH *adds the champagne bottle and two glasses to the tray, then turns to the door*)

HUGH. Right, there we are. Two glasses, pot of caviare, nice warm spoon, champagne. Good night, darling.

LIZ. Hugh . . .

HUGH (*stepping back to her, still*) Yes?

LIZ. Shut the door—I want to talk to you.

(HUGH *shuts the door, and turns round, holding the tray*)

HUGH. I don't think there's much left to say.

LIZ. Put that tray down—you look too silly carrying it. (*This repetition is due to her frayed nerves*)

HUGH. I'm all right, thanks.

(*He remains standing, holding it. She nearly loses her temper, but decides not to*)

Well, what's on your mind?

LIZ. You—making a fool of yourself.

HUGH. Me?

LIZ (*moving below the sofa to the fire*) Yes—you—taking caviare and champagne upstairs to a girl, at your age.

HUGH (*moving c*). Never mind my age. It's hers that matters.

LIZ. If the whole thing wasn't so pathetically ridiculous, I'd laugh. But as it is, I merely feel like crying.

HUGH. Cry away—It'll do you good, my darling.

LIZ (*again repetitive*) You're behaving like a spoilt child.

HUGH (*looking down at the tray*) Really! I must be a thoroughly precocious one, in that case! Listen, I'm providing evidence for you. Please don't think that I wouldn't rather take up a jug of hot water and two aspirins. At my age, it's no joke—this kind of thing—like fielding in the Fathers' Match at long leg at Dick's private school. Will that be all—or do you want to go on being beastly to me?

LIZ. I'm not being beastly to you, Hugh.

HUGH. In that case, I'll put down my tray. (*He puts the tray on the sofa table*)

LIZ. I'm trying to make you see sense, that's all. You won't do any good by going on like this.

HUGH. It's worth a try, though, isn't it?

LIZ (*moving to Hugh c*) No—I've made up my mind—and nothing's going to change it. I'm in love with John, and John's in love with me—and there's precisely nothing you can do about it— anyone can do about it. I'm so sorry, Hugh—but these things happen—you admitted that yourself—they happen and it's no use trying to prevent them.

HUGH (*after a pause*) How hard did you try?

LIZ. Extremely hard—I really did—ask John.

HUGH. I'll take your word for it. (*He pauses*) You don't think if I wore a cummerbund . . .?

LIZ. No, darling.

HUGH. What about a term or two at Gordonstoun or somewhere? You know, shinning up Ben Nevis on a nylon rope—or jumping off a cliff and chasing the Sports Master under water . . .

LIZ (*moving down* R, *her lips twitching, trying to hide it from him*) I'm not laughing.

HUGH. What about a course of monkey glands, then? (*Moving down* C) I'm told they do wonders. It'd only take a fortnight, and when you got back from Italy you'd find me swinging through the branches in the garden, howling for my mate.

LIZ. I'm still not laughing.

HUGH. That's the trouble—where's it got to?

LIZ. What?

HUGH. Your sense of humour?

LIZ. Love's no laughing matter, darling. That's one reason why all this has happened, actually—you've always thought it was.

HUGH. It could be—couldn't it?

LIZ. Not for a woman, no.

HUGH. You laughed that night I fell out of bed on our honeymoon in Avignon, and cut my backside on a tooth-glass.

LIZ. I know I did.

HUGH. Well?

LIZ. One can't live on that for fifteen years.

HUGH. I could give a repeat performance if pressed. Has John ever laughed?

LIZ. Of course he has.

HUGH. No—I mean in the mews flat—behind the red velvet curtains?

LIZ. Never you mind.

HUGH (*moving* RC) That means "no". Oh, my poor darling—and you want to live with that for ever—you'll be sewing a crêpe border round your nightgown next!

LIZ (*moving up to the door*) If you're going on like this, I'll say good night.

HUGH. Well, *honi soit qui mal y pense.* (*He goes to pick up his tray*)

LIZ. Hugh—you aren't really serious?

HUGH (*with the tray*) I am, my dear—I'm going right through with it, if it kills me. (*He walks towards the door*) I want you two going off to Italy without a worry in the world—in the full knowledge that I've given you your evidence, and you can marry John the moment the divorce comes through. I'll ring young Rubinstein on Monday morning and get him to start the ball rolling. (*He has reached the door, and stops in front of her*) I'll call it off if you'll stay with me.

LIZ. I don't like blackmail.

HUGH. All right, then—forget about the blackmail and just stay with me.

LIZ. I can't.

HUGH. Why not?

LIZ. Because I love John.

HUGH. O.K. Turn the lights out, will you? Good night, darling—wish me luck.

(LIZ *moves* R. HUGH *steps into the doorway and turns*)

And if I should holler in the night, don't hesitate to dial nine-nine-nine!

CURTAIN

SCENE 2

SCENE—*The same. The following morning, a fine day. Breakfast is set for four on the table* R, *and three chairs placed round it.*

When the CURTAIN *rises,* MRS GRAY *is discovered setting out coffee on the sofa table.* JOHN *enters up* LC, *dressed for travelling, and moves up* L *of the sofa.*

JOHN. Good morning, Mrs Gray. (*He picks up the "Sunday Times" from the sofa arm*)

MRS GRAY. Good morning, Mr Brownlow. Breakfast's ready and the coffee's nice and hot.

JOHN. Good. Thank you. Mrs Walford down yet? (*He moves to the desk*)

MRS GRAY. She went off to Early Service, sir.

JOHN. Oh, did she? (*He puts a section of the paper on the desk, then moves to the french windows*) What a lovely day. By Jove—that border's looking wonderful.

MRS GRAY (*moving* C) Can't you talk to him, sir?

JOHN. Talk to who? (*He moves* R *of Mrs Gray*)

MRS GRAY. Mr Walford. It's not right—and you're a man. And men talk to each other easier than women do. And you're a friend of Mrs Walford's, aren't you?

JOHN. Yes, indeed.

MRS GRAY. Is that why you're taking her to Italy—to get her right away from him?

JOHN. Well, I suppose you could put it like that.

MRS GRAY. It's not right. Mrs Walford's always been a good wife to him—never looked to right or left—not since I've known her. And that's fifteen years. We came here—Mr Gray and me—the week they got back from their honeymoon. And, ever since then, it's been such a happy place—him with his books—her with her garden and the children. Well, of course, they've had their ups and downs—who hasn't in the writing world! I've seen him so down sometimes I've been worried for him—but she's always cheered him up and got him writing again. And now this—I don't know what's come over him, I really don't. I said to Mr Gray last night, "I don't know what's come over him", I said.

(JOHN, *hoping to divert the flow, moves to the sofa table and helps himself to breakfast.* LIZ *enters through the french windows, unseen by either of them*)

And he said, "Maybe there's more to it than you think, Jean". "Well", I said, "I hope not, Jim, it's bad enough already". That was last night. Then, when I took up the tea at half-past seven to the spare room, and I saw him and that hussy sitting up in bed together— bold as brass—with one arm round her shoulder and the other . . .

(JOHN *turns round with his plate and coffee to take his seat at the table, and sees Liz*)

JOHN. Hullo, Liz. (*He moves to the table and sits* R)
LIZ. Good morning, John. Good morning, Mrs Gray.
MRS GRAY. Good morning, Ma'am—breakfast's all ready.
LIZ. Thank you.

(MRS GRAY *goes towards the door with her empty tray.* LIZ *looks at John, and makes up her mind*)

Mrs Gray . . .
MRS GRAY. Yes, Ma'am?
LIZ. I overheard what you were saying then to Mr Brownlow.
MRS GRAY. Yes—I was afraid you had, Ma'am, and I'm sorry.
LIZ. Don't be. It was no surprise to me. And thank you for your indignation and support—but it's misplaced. I've got to tell her, John—I'm sorry. But it isn't fair to Hugh to let her think like that. It's my fault, Mrs Gray—entirely—Mr Walford's blameless.
MRS GRAY. Blameless!
LIZ. Well, let's say he's not to blame initially. (*She moves* L *of John and puts her hand on his shoulder*) The fact is that I started it. I fell in love with Mr Brownlow and he fell in love with me and, when the divorce comes through, we're getting married.
MRS GRAY. Jim was right, then, after all.
LIZ. Jim?
MRS GRAY. Mr Gray—I've just been telling Mr Brownlow he was telling me last night there might be more to it than what I thought.
LIZ. Yes, Jim was right.
MRS GRAY. I don't know what to say, dear.
LIZ (*moving* RC) Well, perhaps that's just as well, because I don't suppose you think a great deal of me—after what I've told you.
MRS GRAY. If it's love, dear—I'm not blaming you. Because it can't be helped. There's nothing anyone can do about it—not a woman anyway. I learnt that when I married Jim. I couldn't stand the sight of him—not for a minute—but I loved him so I married him.

(MRS GRAY *exits.* LIZ *closes the door*)

LIZ (*returning to John*) I'm sorry, John—that must have been embarrassing for you.
JOHN (*rising*) For me—what about you! When you came in—and

heard all that about the tea tray! (*He takes her hand*) How was Early Service?

LIZ. All right. Darling, did you mind me telling Mrs Gray?

JOHN. No, I feel better now it's out.

LIZ (*going over to the sofa table*) Yes, so do I.

JOHN. Poor Jim—she does talk, doesn't she?

LIZ. Yes, she's a dear, though. (*She picks up the coffee-pot*)

(JOHN *eats his breakfast.* LIZ *suddenly puts down the coffee-pot, her shoulders heaving silently—then she bursts into violent sobs. He hears her, and jumps up*)

JOHN (*moving to LIZ*) Liz, my darling—what's the matter?

LIZ. Nothing—leave me alone, darling. I'll be all right in a minute. Please sit down and go on with your breakfast—I'll be all right. Please.

(*As* JOHN *moves away* LIZ *whips round, furiously*)

How could he, John—how could he! In his own home, with that girl—in front of Mrs Gray. How could he!

JOHN (*sitting as before*) Well, he told you he was going to, didn't he?

LIZ (*moving to John*) Yes, but I never thought he meant it—did you?

JOHN. P'raps he didn't.

LIZ. What do you mean?

JOHN. P'raps he really didn't mean it.

LIZ. Don't tell me it happened by mistake.

JOHN. Perhaps it didn't happen.

LIZ. But she saw them.

JOHN. In bed, yes—but what does that prove?

LIZ (*moving* C) Quite enough for a Divorce Court Judge.

JOHN. Ah, yes, exactly—that's what I mean.

LIZ. You mean Hugh got into bed just before Mrs Gray brought in that tea tray?

JOHN. Well, it's not impossible.

LIZ. Would you have?

JOHN (*after a pause*) Darling—what a question!

LIZ (*moving to John*) Would you have, John?

JOHN. No—not in the circumstances.

LIZ. In what circumstances?

JOHN. Well, the set-up. (*Rising and moving to the sofa table*) Wife unfaithful—damned attractive girl. I would have taken full advantage of it, I'm afraid. But I'm not Hugh.

LIZ. What do you mean by that?

JOHN. Well, we're different. He said so himself last night. My wave-length's physical, and his is mental—broadly speaking—that's what he said. And he also said his batteries were running down.

LIZ. He said that?

JOHN. Yes—through old age—lack of distilled water, and a little too much distilled whisky.

(LIZ *moves down* R, *and her mouth twitches, unseen by John*)

So, don't worry, darling—not that you've the smallest right to, as I told you last night. It was all a put-up job. He nipped in from the dressing-room, beating the tea tray by a short head.

LIZ. But I listened at the dressing-room door, last night—and he wasn't in there.

JOHN. How do you know?

LIZ. Well, he wasn't snoring.

JOHN (*moving above the sofa and down* L) P'raps he had a night off. Don't be silly, darling. He went in this morning, just before the maid came in in the approved style.

LIZ. That was seven-thirty.

JOHN (*moving in to the sofa*) Yes—that's what I'm saying.

LIZ. Well, it's half-past nine now, and he's not down yet.

JOHN (*sitting on the sofa*) He's dressing, darling—don't be silly.

LIZ. Well, let's hope so.

(HUGH *enters, in his Jaeger dressing-gown and carpet slippers, and gay as a cricket*)

HUGH. Morning, Liz, good morning, John. (*He moves to the window*)

JOHN (*rising*) Good morning. (*He sits*)

HUGH (*looking into the garden*) Isn't it a lovely day—you'll have a perfect crossing to Le Touquet.

(LIZ *picks up the coffee from the sofa table, goes to the table* R *and sits* L *of it*)

So will Molly, bless her, in her little Channel steamer. (*He moves to the sofa table*) What time are you going, darling?

(LIZ *makes no reply*)

JOHN. Half an hour.

HUGH. Oh, well, there isn't any violent hurry. What's old Ma Gray trundled up for breakfast? I could eat an ox. All packed up, darling?

LIZ. Yes, thanks.

HUGH. Good. And you, John?

JOHN. Yes.

HUGH (*helping himself to breakfast*) Good. All the little bits and pieces? Cuff links—shaving soap—ties—dressing-gown—cords—toothbrush—cummerbunds—you get them all in?

JOHN. Yes, I think so.

HUGH (*moving* R *with his plate*) Well done—what about you, darling? Bras—bikinis—nylons—Metatone—suspender belts—

foundation cream—eight dozen pairs of shoes—hair-curlers—
Kleenex—all in order?

LIZ. Yes, Hugh, thank you.

HUGH. What's the matter, darling—had a bad night?

LIZ. No, I'm quite all right, Hugh.

HUGH. Good. Sleep well, John? (*He sits above the table*)

JOHN. Yes, thanks.

HUGH. Well done. What time are you due in Milan?

JOHN. Eight tomorrow morning.

HUGH. Oh, good. You'll see the mountains in the early morning
from the window of the couchette when you're snaking down to
Milan. I'm referring to the train, old boy.

(*There is a long pause, as he eats his breakfast*)

Are the berths in a couchette, one above the other?

JOHN. I'm not sure—I think so.

HUGH. Which do you prefer? I like the top one myself.

JOHN. So do I.

HUGH. That's lucky. Liz prefers the bottom one, don't you, my
darling? Always has. I've never understood why. All you get down
there's a close-up of a pair of hairy legs and flat feet, shinning up a
ladder. Whereas, on the top, you've got a bit of privacy—apart from
pairs of trousers on coat-hangers clipping you across the jaw at
intervals.

(MOLLY *enters in a dressing-gown, again looking a dish*)

(*Rising and moving to the sofa table*) Ah, there you are, my darling—
come along and help yourself.

MOLLY (*moving to the sofa table*) Good morning, Mrs Walford.

HUGH. Molly said "Good morning", Liz. (*He returns to his seat*)

LIZ (*rising and moving* RC) What—oh, good morning—I'm so sorry,
I was thinking about something else.

MOLLY. Good morning, John.

JOHN (*rising*) Good morning, Molly. (*He moves to the fireplace*)

MOLLY. Isn't it a lovely morning. I feel I could eat a horse. (*She
goes over to the sofa table*)

HUGH. Remember that your train's at ten-five, darling.

MOLLY. That's all right—I've packed.

HUGH (*moving to Molly*) Well, as I'm going to run you to the
station, I'll nip up and get dressed. (*To Molly*) No hurry, dear—you
haven't got to shave, but I have. See you again, John—before you go.
I'll be down in a jiffy. Gray'll bring the luggage down, if you ring,
darling. (*He moves to the door*)

(MOLLY *goes to the table with her breakfast and sits* R)

LIZ. All right, Hugh.

HUGH. And make sure that you've packed the Metatone.

(HUGH *exits.* LIZ *moves to the desk*)

JOHN (*to Molly*) You're going to have a nice, smooth crossing.

MOLLY. Yes, I think so. You're flying to Le Touquet, aren't you?

JOHN. Yes, and then we catch the car-train at Boulogne. I don't suppose you go on that one.

MOLLY. No, mine's passenger.

JOHN. Of course—it would be—if you haven't got a car.

LIZ. I'm going to go and get my things together, darling.

JOHN. Right.

LIZ. Good-bye, Miss Forsyth—just in case you're upstairs, getting ready.

MOLLY. Good-bye, Mrs Walford—thank you so much. I've enjoyed it so much—it was sweet of you to have me.

LIZ. Not at all—I'm so glad you could come. I hope you'll have a lovely holiday.

MOLLY. Thanks so much.

LIZ. John, time's getting on.

JOHN. I know.

(LIZ *exits*)

JOHN (*turning to Molly*) It's all bluff, isn't it?

MOLLY. What is?

JOHN. You're not the girl that you pretend you are—and Hugh pretends you are.

MOLLY. What kind of girl is that?

JOHN. "The kind of girl that goes right through the office like a circular"—I quote.

MOLLY. Who told you that?

JOHN (*moving to the table* R) Well, Hugh told Liz—and she repeated it to me. Tell me it isn't true.

MOLLY. What does it matter to you—one way or the other?

JOHN (*sitting above the table*) I'm incurably romantic.

MOLLY. You'd prefer me to have had a dozen husbands—rather than a string of lovers?

JOHN. Definitely.

MOLLY (*rising and moving to the sofa table*) What a Puritan you are. You should have been a Covenanting Minister in Scotland in the old days—doing dreadful things behind the shelter of the law.

JOHN. So you think I do dreadful things?

MOLLY. Well—running off with Liz.

JOHN. I am in love with her, you know.

MOLLY. So's Hugh.

JOHN. I'll have to take your word for it.

MOLLY. You don't believe me?

JOHN. Well, let's say he doesn't shout it round the market-place.

MOLLY. You think he should?

JOHN. If he wanted to keep her—yes. I think it would have been wise.

MOLLY. He's not ostentatious. (*She sits* L *on the sofa*)

John. You're telling me.

Molly. No. He's unselfish. Liz's happiness comes first with him—and not his own. If he's decided she'll be happier with you, that's all that matters.

John. So he lets her go without a fight.

Molly. I don't suppose he thinks that fighting leads to happiness.

John. That's not the way to keep a woman.

Molly. It could be the way to keep one happy, though.

John. I'd question if he's made her happy recently.

Molly. Until you met her, I'd say he managed quite well.

John (*rising and moving to the fire*) I don't mean that. I mean in this house since we arrived here yesterday. I wouldn't say that his behaviour—with you last night, for example—was conspicuously geared to make her happy.

Molly. He was helping over the divorce.

John. By having tea with you in bed this morning!

Molly. Yes.

John. You're pretty brazen, aren't you?

Molly. I'd rather use the word "straightforward". (*She rises and moves to the sofa table*) It's more flattering. And, anyway, what right have you to criticize me? The divorce'll go through now, provided Mrs Gray does her stuff—and you don't get caught by the Queen's Proctor out in Italy and he starts intervening.

(John *looks at her interestedly.* Molly *notices this and continues somewhat automatically*)

I think that's a lovely word, don't you? I visualize a little man in horn rims and a bowler hat, creeping down corridors in car-trains—intervening madly all night.

John (*moving* LC) You look smashing in that dressing-gown.

Molly. You said that quite mechanically.

John. Oh, did I?

Molly. Yes—like one of those machines on railway platforms—(*sitting on the* R *arm of the sofa*)—slip a woman in the slot and watch it turning out a platitude.

John. You get more charming every minute.

Molly. That's much better. That came out quite naturally—although you didn't mean it—and it therefore sounded quite sincere! I'm sorry for you, John.

John. Sorry for me!

Molly. Yes—I find you pathetic.

John. Thank you very much.

Molly (*rising and moving* C) Well, look at you, three honeymoons at your age and another in the offing! (*She moves up* C) Talk about commuting! You don't need a marriage licence—what you want's a season ticket!

John (*sitting on the armchair above the fire*) So you disapprove of my divorces?

MOLLY. No, your marriages. You never should have married any of them.

JOHN. Oh, why not?

MOLLY. Because you didn't love them.

JOHN. On the contrary, I did.

MOLLY. All right then, you did, but for the wrong reasons. (*She sits on the* L *arm of the sofa*) Perfect ones for an affair, I'll grant you that. But not for marriage. That's why I'm not married. I'm still looking for a man that I can love for the right reasons.

JOHN. Such as?

MOLLY. Humour—kindness—mutual affection—understanding —tolerance.

JOHN. Like Hugh.

MOLLY. No, not like Hugh. I don't love Hugh that way. But Liz does. And that's why you won't do any better with her than you have done with the other three.

JOHN. I love Liz.

MOLLY. Yes, of course you do—but only physically. And that's the way she loves you too. And that's the trouble. You're like two people playing bridge with far too many trumps between them and too few outside tricks in the other suits. It makes it very difficult to get one's contract.

JOHN (*rising and moving* RC) It depends how well one plays, I should imagine.

MOLLY. I dare say—but you've already lost three rubbers in those circumstances, haven't you.

JOHN. Why are you laughing at me?

MOLLY. Well, why not? It's high time someone did. (*Rising and moving down* L) The truth is that you definitely shouldn't have a wife who loves you physically. You see, you love yourself enough for two already—and a wife who loves you physically makes three—and three's a crowd!

JOHN. Do you write Hugh's books for him?

MOLLY (*moving to John*) What you need's a woman who can laugh at you—and sew your buttons on—and do the ordering. Instead of turning into a blancmange each time you look at her! I know you think there's no such woman in the world. But you should have a look around you just to make sure.

JOHN (*moving down* R) I'm surprised that you don't run a marriage agency.

MOLLY. Well, your account'd be worth having, wouldn't it!

(HUGH *enters*)

HUGH (*in the doorway*) Now, come along, you two, it's zero hour. Good God, you're not dressed yet?

MOLLY (*moving to Hugh*) Oh dear—how long have I got?

HUGH (*looking at his watch*) Fifteen minutes.

MOLLY. Well, good-bye John—if I miss you.

John. Good-bye, Molly.
Hugh (*moving to the armchair above the fire*) Gray'll bring your case down.
Molly. Thank you.

(Molly *exits*)

John (*moving to the door*) I'd better go, too.
Hugh. What time are you leaving?
John. Any time now. I'll nip up and get cracking. (*He moves to Hugh*) Hugh . . .
Hugh. Yes?
John. Sorry about all this.
Hugh. That's all right, old fellow. These things happen.
John. I'll look after her all right.
Hugh. I hope so.
John. And I'll stick to her.
Hugh. Good show. (*He crosses to the table R*)
John. I know you don't believe me—you think it's just physical. It's not, though—it's for the right reasons.
Hugh. Such as?
John (*moving to Hugh*) Humour, kindness, mutual affection, understanding, tolerance . . .
Hugh. I'm glad to hear it.
John. I'll prove it to you.
Hugh. That's right. That's the idea. Run along, or you'll miss your Skyways.

(John *turns for the door again*)

John . . .

(John *turns*)

John. Yes?
Hugh. Don't let her forget the Metatone—morning and evening —one dessert spoon, in a glass of water.

(Liz *enters, wearing a hat and carrying a small case*)

Liz. John, it's nearly time to go. (*She puts down the case and hat*)
John. Right, darling—I'll be with you in five minutes.

(John *exits*)

Liz. Well, good-bye, Hugh.
Hugh. Good-bye, old girl.
Liz. You'll tell the children, won't you?
Hugh. Yes, of course. Dick's coming out from school next week-end. I'll tell him then.
Liz. And Sheila?
Hugh. I'll go down and see her during the week.
Liz. Please don't make me out too awful.

HUGH. Why should I do that, my darling?

LIZ. What excuses will you make for me?

HUGH. None. I'll just tell the truth.

LIZ (*moving* LC) You're good at doing that, too, aren't you?

HUGH. Well, I do my best.

LIZ. In that case, p'raps you'll tell me where you spent last night.

HUGH. What purpose would that serve?

LIZ. I want to know.

HUGH. Why?

LIZ. Because I'm a woman.

HUGH (*moving* C) So is Molly.

LIZ. I dare say—but you've already told me she's accommodating —so what's wrong with telling me about the latest chapter? I told you about John.

HUGH. No, you didn't—Molly did.

LIZ. I told you about the mews flat, then.

HUGH. No—you didn't. I told you.

LIZ. Well, I confirmed it.

HUGH. Granted.

LIZ. Then it's only fair you should confirm this.

HUGH. I'm afraid I disagree. The mews flat was a basic piece of puzzle in the jig-saw of our marriage. Last night, thanks to the incredibly broad base of the divorce laws in this country—was irrelevant. The only thing that matters was that Mrs Gray saw us in bed together, drinking China tea and eating Rich Tea biscuits. Anything that happened before that—or after that—or both—is quite beside the point. I've given you the evidence for the divorce—that's all that matters. You'd better tell Gray if you want to take your golf clubs.

LIZ (*moving down* L) I have told him.

HUGH (*moving to the armchair down* R *and sitting*) Good. (*After a pause*) John's going to bore your pants clean off.

LIZ. What makes you think so?

HUGH. He does.

LIZ. He's not in the least bit boring.

HUGH. Maybe not in bed. But you can't stay in bed for ever—not unless you're an invalid. In which case, you're better off in bed alone! He's a bore my darling Liz—a great big cracking bore. He hasn't got an idea in his head, except one—and it's not a new one. It's been going on since Adam knocked off gardening and started talking to that very superficial serpent. And it's not a basis for the future.

LIZ (*moving down* C) I'd have thought that history'd contradicted that for some time.

HUGH. Only population-wise—and any given pair of rabbits can do better, if it comes to that. (*Moving* C) I'm talking about plain, straightforward sex, my darling, with or without an end-product, and it's not the same as marriage, which is less enjoyable, I dare say, but a great deal more rewarding in the long run and most definitely not a thing to be embarked on lightly—that's why rabbits have no time for it—I should imagine.

Liz (*moving down* R) What's all this in aid of, Hugh—your new book?

Hugh. I'm not saying I won't use it later—but it's aimed at you just at the moment.

Liz. Well, I'm afraid it's not hitting the mark.

Hugh (*sitting on the* L *arm of the sofa*) A pity. If you weren't so infatuated it would. You'd realize that although Johnski may be a prize rabbit with the walls of his hutch papered with rosettes, he's also going to be a wash-out as a husband.

Liz. Give me one good reason.

Hugh. Certainly. He's got no sense of humour. If he fell out of bed and cut himself on a tooth-glass he wouldn't laugh. He'd stick a Band-aid on it and go back to square one. Life's too short to spend it with a fellow like that!

Liz (*cutting in*) Can I get a word in edgeways?

Hugh. Please do.

Liz. Thank you. (*Moving above and round the sofa, and returning down* R) Every word you say displays your ignorance of women and of life in general. I don't know how you've got away with it for all these years. I really don't. But just because the cardboard figures in your silly little books say cardboard things, you think you're Socrates, or someone—whereas in reality you've no more idea of what love is to a woman than a monk has.

Hugh (*half to himself*) Abelard?

Liz. You see that's you all over—always trying to be funny. Here you are, saying good-bye to someone you've been married to for fifteen years and all you do is make facetious little literary cracks like some dehydrated old Don. (*She sits down* R)

Hugh. I'm sorry, but it slipped out when you started talking about monks. And Abelard was the first one that came into my head. You've read the book, of course.

Liz. You read it to me.

Hugh. So I did. You didn't mean that sort of monk, though, did you?

Liz. No, I didn't.

Hugh. You meant the conventional kind—beads and gardening and Bible—reading during meals—and great big bare toes, flapping up and down like croissants.

(Liz's *lips twitch*)

P'raps I'd better take the veil—or whatever it is that monks do. (*He moves round* L *of the sofa to* C) Maybe that's my future, darling—tending vines on top of some hot mountain, in a dressing-gown, and getting plastered alone in my cell on Saint's day. Will you come and see me, darling, sometimes? Just to keep me up to date on Dick and

Sheila and the Derby winner and John's latest dirty story from the Stock Exchange? Oh, well, it's no use talking—he'll be down in a minute. So, if you're determined on it, I can only wish you luck. And, as I say, I've given you the evidence for the divorce—and so it's all plain sailing. (*He walks away to the desk to get a cigarette. She looks at him, and makes up her mind*)

Liz. I don't want one.

Hugh (*turning to Liz*) What did you say?

Liz. I don't want a divorce.

Hugh. Why not?

Liz (*moving down* L) You know why not perfectly well.

Hugh. Because John lacks humour?

Liz. No, because you've got too much. You've killed it, Hugh.

Hugh. Killed what—I don't like killing things.

Liz. My love for John. It's dead. It died the moment you found out about it. And you buried it the moment that you asked him down here, and I saw you both together. And you stuck the tombstone in position last night.

Hugh. Last night?

Liz. When you talked about your monkey glands, and when you went up to the spare room dressing-room with caviare and champagne on that beastly little tray. You made it all seem sordid—in a moment. What had been so beautiful before—so secret and so precious and so heavenly—you made a joke of. It became just every day and commonplace—the sort of thing that other people do and keep on doing all the time in beastly little flats and hotels up and down the country when it's raining. Fat, complaisant men in sock-suspenders and huge leather belts like hoops and hard-faced women taking off suspender belts like someone ripping plaster off a boil. It all became so sordid, and you killed it, Hugh.

Hugh (*after a pause*) I'm sorry, darling.

Liz. Never mind—it can't be helped—it's done now. (*She goes and picks up the hat*)

Hugh. So you're going to stay at home with me?

Liz (*moving* c) Yes, if you'll have me.

Hugh. I'll have you, darling. You're certain, are you?

Liz. Yes, Hugh.

Hugh. You won't change your mind again.

Liz. No, never.

Hugh. Then why are you putting on that bloody silly hat?

Liz (*moving down* L) Because I'm still going off to Italy with John, but I'm not going to marry him. You've killed my love for him, all right, but you can't stop me finding him attractive. So, I'm going off to Italy.

Hugh (*moving up* c) To have an affair with him?

Liz (*defiantly*) Yes.

Hugh. Like all those other people in the rain?

Liz. It won't be raining.

HUGH. You're not, you know.

LIZ. I am, Hugh.

HUGH. No—you're not. Or, if you do, you won't be seeing me again.

LIZ. You mean that you won't have me back?

HUGH. That's right.

LIZ. But why not?

HUGH. Because I won't want you.

LIZ. You won't want me!

HUGH (*moving up* R) No—and I'll tell you why—because I've found a substitute—the perfect substitute. A pretty girl who loves me for all the right reasons. And, what's more, she's got a sense of humour.

LIZ. And I haven't?

HUGH. No. (*Moving* C) You had one once, I'll grant you—but you've lost it, since that dinner with the Chilean Ambassador. And I can't live with somebody who hasn't got a sense of humour.

LIZ. You propose to live with Molly?

HUGH. If she'll have me.

LIZ. Marry her, you mean?

HUGH. Why not?

LIZ. You're old enough to be her father.

HUGH. What's that got to do with it?

LIZ. It's laughable.

HUGH (*moving to the sofa*) That's just why the idea appeals to me so much. (*He sits*)

LIZ. You've gone mad, Hugh.

HUGH. No, I don't think so—merely been rejuvenated. Nothing like a shake-up when you're in a rut. And we've been in one now for seven or eight years, my darling, and I've managed to climb out of it, thank God. Time's getting on—we'd better call the others, or they'll miss all their connections.

LIZ (*moving* C) So that's final is it? You won't have me back?

HUGH. Not on your terms, no.

LIZ. On what terms, then?

HUGH. If you take that silly hat off, and give up your trip to Italy, I'll think about it.

LIZ. Think about it—is that all?

HUGH. It's something, isn't it?

(LIZ *moves down* R, *irresolute*)

I'll finish my book in a week or two. Then I thought I might push off on a holiday.

(LIZ *half hears this*)

Would you like to come with me?

(LIZ *looks round, blankly, at him*)

We could drop in on Avignon and find out if they've replaced that tooth-glass yet!

(LIZ *turns away to hide her smile.* HUGH *watches her.* JOHN *enters and moves down to Liz*)

JOHN. Well, here we are, my darling—dead on time. Gray's put your cases in the car.

(Liz, *after a second takes of her hat*)

HUGH. Well he'd better take them out again.

(JOHN *looks up*)

LIZ. John, I'm not going.
JOHN. What! You're pulling my leg!
LIZ. No—I'm not, John.
JOHN (*moving* C) Here—what's going on?
HUGH. She's changed her mind, old fellow—that's all—women do, you know.
JOHN (*moving to Liz*) Is that right darling?
LIZ. Yes, John.
JOHN. But—why?
LIZ. I don't know—don't ask me, please.
JOHN. But you still love me, don't you?
LIZ. Yes, but not for the right reasons.
JOHN (*moving to the desk*) Oh, my God.

(MOLLY *comes in, dressed for the road, and moves* C)

(*Moving to Molly*) Have you been talking to Liz?
MOLLY. No—apart from saying good-bye. Why, what's happened?
JOHN. You tell me.
HUGH. She's going to stay with me, and see how things work out.
MOLLY (*moving to Liz*) I'm so glad.
LIZ. You—glad?
MOLLY. Yes, why not?
LIZ. Aren't you in love with Hugh?
MOLLY. Not so you'd notice.
LIZ. You mean that you wouldn't marry him if he proposed to you?
MOLLY. Of course not.
LIZ. But why not—Hugh said . . .
MOLLY. Because it wouldn't be for the right reasons. (*She moves up to the desk*)
JOHN. If I hear that phrase again, I'll scream.
HUGH. You'll miss your plane, John—if you don't get moving.
JOHN (*moving down* R *to Liz*) Come on, Liz—he's bluffing. He's been leading you a dance. All he's been doing is to try to make you jealous. He's succeeded, I admit—but now his bluff's been called. (*Pulling Liz by the wrist to* RC) So let's get moving.
LIZ. No, John.

JOHN. But, why not?

LIZ. I can't explain—I've told you. Don't keep asking questions. (*She moves down* R) I'm not coming—that's all.

JOHN. Well, in that case, I'd better say good-bye.

LIZ. Are you still going off to Italy without me?

JOHN. Yes, I've got to. I've got business in Milan.

LIZ. Business in Milan—yes, of course you have. Good-bye, John.

JOHN. Aren't you going to kiss me?

(LIZ *looks at Hugh.* HUGH *nods*)

LIZ. All right. (*She moves to John*)

JOHN. Good-bye, darling.

(JOHN *and* LIZ *kiss*)

HUGH (*rising and moving to John*) Bye-bye, Johnski. Thanks for coming down. It was a great help.

JOHN. Good-bye, Molly.

MOLLY. Good-bye, John.

(JOHN *starts to go to the door*)

HUGH. Why don't you drop her at the station—just outside the lodge gate?

JOHN. All right.

MOLLY. Are you sure you don't mind?

JOHN. No—of course not. We'd better go, though. It's just on ten.

(JOHN *exits*)

MOLLY (*moving to Liz*) Well, good-bye, Mrs Walford.

LIZ. Good-bye, Molly.

MOLLY. Good-bye, Mr Walford. (*She turns for the door*)

HUGH. Aren't you going to kiss me?

MOLLY. All right. (*She kisses him*) Good-bye, Hugh.

HUGH. Good-bye, my darling.

(MOLLY *exits.* LIZ *moves to the window. There is the sound of a car revving up and driving away.* HUGH *goes to the door and calls*)

(*calling*) Mrs Gray!

(MRS GRAY *enters*)

MRS GRAY. Yes, Mr Walford?

HUGH. Ah yes, Mrs Gray. Could you ask Mr Gray if he'd take Mrs Walford's suitcase upstairs to her room again?

MRS GRAY. Yes, sir.

HUGH. And could you move my things back from the spare room dressing-room into my own, please?

MRS GRAY. Yes, sir. And will you both be lunching at home?

HUGH. Yes, I think so. (*He looks at Liz*) Won't we, darling?

(LIZ *does not reply*)

That's right—both at home for lunch. Thanks so much, Mrs Gray.

(MRS GRAY *exits.* LIZ *stands looking out of the window, still—after the car.*

HUGH *goes to the desk and picks up the playing cards*)

We're one game all. (*He replaces the cards, picks up the card-table from behind the drinks table, unfolds it and places it in front of the sofa. He goes to the desk for the cards, then to the table* R *for a chair which he puts* L *of the card-table. He sits on the chair and cuts the cards—one pile on Liz's place, one on his own*) So let's have the decider.

(LIZ *moves to the sofa and sits. They start to play, then* LIZ's *shoulders heave, and she starts sobbing*)

Don't cry, please. Please don't cry, darling. (*He rises and sits* L *of her on the sofa*) He's the wrong man for you. He's not on your wavelength. Or if he is, it's a pirate station. He'd have ditched you in a few years, if not earlier. You don't believe me, do you? All right, I'll have to prove it to you. (*He goes to the telephone and dials*)

(LIZ *stops crying, out of interest*)

(*On the telephone*) Hullo, that the station? . . . Ah yes, good. Good morning. Mr Walford here. Tell me—did someone from here drop a lady for the ten-five—very pretty, in a lemon-coloured coat? . . . Nobody . . . And the ten-five's gone out, has it? . . . It has. I see. Thank you. I'm so sorry to have troubled you on such a lovely morning. Good-bye. (*He hangs up and returns to the card-table. He gathers up his cards and hers. Then he puts her cards in her hand gently*) I think we'd better start again, don't you?

HUGH *begins to shuffle. So does* LIZ, *as—*

the CURTAIN *falls*

FURNITURE AND PROPERTY LIST

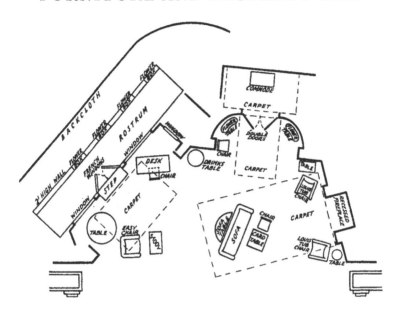

ACT I

SCENE I

On stage: Small table (down L). *On it:* cigarettes, matches, ashtray, vase
Louis Tub chair (down L)
Louis Tub chair (above fireplace)
Table (up L). *On it:* lamp, photographs of Sheila and Dick
2 oval tables (either side of door). *On them:* flower vases
Small chair (up C)
Drinks table (up C). *On it:* lamp, tray of glasses, whisky and
    sherry decanters, bottle of gin, tonic water, jug of water, bottle
    opener, ashtray, cigarettes
Desk (up R). *On it:* writing materials, telephone, lamp, photo-
    graphs. *In drawer:* traveller's cheques, passport
Waste-paper basket (under desk)
Desk chair (below desk)
Circular table (down R). *On it:* lamp, vase of flowers, ashtray
Easy chair (down R)

Stool (down RC)

Sofa (LC). *On it:* cushions

Sofa table. *On it:* ashtray, cigarettes, lighter, magazines, bowl of
flowers

Card-table (below sofa). *On it:* cards laid for "Racing Demon",
cigarettes, matches, ashtray, pad, pencil

Small chair (above card-table)

Commode (in hall)

Carpets

Window curtains

SCENE 2

Strike: Card-table
Dirty glasses
Stool
Bowls of flowers from R table and sofa table

Set: R table further on stage. *On it:* a small bowl of flowers, leaves,
wrapping paper. *Under it:* waste-paper basket from desk
Plate of nuts on sofa table
On drinks table: sliced lemon, 4 whisky glasses, 2 sherry glasses
Sofa and sofa table to face more directly downstage
Easy chair to down R corner

Off-stage: Ice bucket (MRS GRAY)
Metatone and caviare in parcels (HUGH)
Sandals (LIZ)
Bouquet of lilies, bouquet of roses (MRS GRAY)
Vase, for lilies (MRS GRAY)
Vase, for roses (MRS GRAY)

Personal: HUGH: watch
JOHN: handkerchief

ACT II
SCENE I

Strike: Roses
Lilies
Metatone
Ice bucket
Dirty glasses
Plate of nuts
Lemon

Set: Card-table below sofa. *On it:* cards set for bridge, 2 bridge pads,
pencils, spare pack of cards
3 chairs around card-table
Card box on L arm of sofa
Cardigan on R arm of sofa

On drinks table: champagne on ice with napkin, spare champagne
bottle, 4 champagne glasses, 1 gin glass, bottle of bitter lemon
Vase of 1 dozen roses on down R table
Stool in front of easy chair
Crumpled card in waste-paper basket

Off-stage: Bouquet of lilies (MRS GRAY)
Pot of caviare and spoon on tray (HUGH)

Personal: JOHN: wallet with 10*s.* note

SCENE 2

Strike: Stool
Champagne bucket and glasses
Table lamp and ashtray from down R table
Everything from sofa table

Set: False table top on table down R with breakfast laid for four
On sofa table: tray with coffee, milk, 2 cups and saucers, hot plate
with 4 breakfast plates, dish of egg and bacon, servers
"Sunday Times" on L arm of sofa
3 chairs round table down R

Personal: LIZ: week-end bag, hat

LIGHTING PLOT

Property fittings required: 4 table lamps, 2 wall brackets.
INTERIOR: A living-room. The same scene throughout.
THE APPARENT SOURCES OF LIGHT are: by day, french windows R; by night,
lamps and wall brackets.
THE MAIN ACTING AREAS are down R, RC, up and down C, LC.

ACT I SCENE 1. Night
To open: Lamps and brackets lit. Moonlight outside windows
Cue 1   HUGH turns off lights   (Page 15)
Snap off all lighting except desk lamp

ACT I SCENE 2. Day
To open: Effect of morning light
No cues

ACT II SCENE 1. Night
To open: As Act I Scene 1
No cues

ACT II Scene 2. Day
To open: Effect of bright sunny morning
No cues

EFFECTS PLOT

ACT I

SCENE 1

Cue 1	HUGH: ". . . not a Moslem" *Sound of distant train*	(Page 12)
Cue 2	HUGH goes to turn off desk lamp *Telephone tinkles*	(Page 15)

SCENE 2

Cue 3	MRS GRAY: ". . . name for it too" *Sound of two cars arriving*	(Page 17)

ACT II

SCENE 1

No cues

SCENE 2

Cue 4	LIZ moves to window *Sound of car revving up and driving away*	(Page 63)
Cue 5	HUGH puts table below sofa *Sound of distant train arriving at station*	(Page 64)
Cue 6	HUGH: "So let's have the decider" *Sound of train departing*	(Page 64)

Lightning Source UK Ltd.
Milton Keynes UK
UKOW07f1015010215

245424UK00001B/5/P